"By drawing from examples in corporate life, the authors show how 'crowd-tapping' and 'crowd-enablement' are already having significant positive impact on innovation, marketing, philanthropy, corporate social responsibility, and social enterprises. Highly recommended."

Professor Alan Barrell, Cambridge University

"A rare insider's look at the cutting edge of some of the world's top companies—and the radical new means they're using to succeed."

Joshua Klein, author of *Reputation Economics*

"Most now 'get it' that crowdfunding will be huge; what this breakthrough book shows is that large companies will be a big part of it, even leading it. Get ready for the stampede as corporate giants discover the myriad benefits of unlocking the power of the crowd."

Jonathan Medved, CEO, OurCrowd

"Crowdfunding and alternative finance generally is enormously disruptive and will make a huge difference to the way private businesses are funded. This book brilliantly examines why this profound transformation is so important."

David Stevenson, Executive Director AltFi
and financial commentator

"Crowdfunding isn't just for startups and social causes, it's about customer engagement, open innovation, and market validation, things every modern company should care about."

Don Tapscott, bestselling author,
most recently of *The Digital Economy*

"Crowdfunding is coming of age and gradually moving into the mainstream. This book spotlights how corporates can leverage crowdfunding and crowdsourcing to amplify marketing, foster innovation, and enhance their CSR programmes. A pioneering and thought-provoking book!"

Bryan Zhang, Crowdfunding and Alternative Finance
Researcher, University of Cambridge

CROWDFUNDING
THE CORPORATE ERA

KEVIN BERG GRELL | DAN MAROM | RICHARD SWART

First published 2015 by
Elliott and Thompson Limited
27 John Street, London WC1N 2BX
www.eandtbooks.com

ISBN: 978-1-78396-161-0

9 8 7 6 5 4 3 2 1

A catalogue record for this book is available from the British Library.

Typesetting: Marie Doherty
Printed in the UK by TJ International Ltd.

CONTENTS

INTRODUCTION
EMPOWERING THE CROWD

Kevin Berg Grell, Dan Marom,
and Richard Swart

The Internet will revolutionize our lives. This might sound like a decades-old slogan, but it is as true today as ever. The Internet is constantly evolving, both in technology and in functionality. Crowdfunding has been hailed as the next Internet revolution. It sprang forth in a time of need, at the end of the last decade, when investors were reticent and financing was scarce. Entrepreneurs, unable to attract a single large influx of capital from a professional investor, decided instead to raise funds in small amounts from a large group of people (the crowd); it was a way of expanding the pool of investors, while also minimizing the risk by spreading it across a multitude of donors. It also made good use of the Internet's potential; campaigns could leverage the power of social media for promotion and communication, and payments could be processed quickly and simply online. It was a method first used in the creative space—for films, plays, and music—and was then adapted for small and medium-sized enterprise finance. Now, as the phenomenon continues to grow exponentially and diversify, it is also evolving—fuelled by technological advancement, regulatory change, and the rapid adaptation of large corporations to collaborative business development.

This book is about the dawn of a new phase in crowdfunding—the era of corporate crowdfunding. When we talk about crowdfunding in this book, we are referring to initiatives where proposals and projects are shared openly, without a specific target customer or investor in mind. In this context, it becomes clear that crowdfunding is about much more than just capital. The crowd is in a sense sourced for information.

Information about public interest is the most crucial piece of information any company—big or small—can obtain. The prospect of better channels through which to gain such information is encouraging large corporations to seek out and execute crowdfunding campaigns alongside small entrepreneurs.

Corporate crowdfunding

Corporate crowdfunding is the use of crowdfunding mechanisms by a corporate entity for the promotion, performance or improvement of one or more of its activities. Although it shares many aspects in common with crowdsourcing, it is not exactly the same thing. Crowdsourcing is the outsourcing of certain functions or activities to the crowd. Corporate crowdfunding adds a crucial layer—one that is built upon small contributions that collectively make a tremendous impact. It weaves crowdsourcing, open innovation and co-creation into a holistic framework for tapping into the resources and wisdom of the crowd.

Clearly, only in rare cases are the funding volumes from crowdfunding platforms anywhere near the needs of a large corporation. When corporations venture into this space it seems clear that they have other motives for doing so. We have identified three areas where corporations can benefit from crowdfunding. These are Marketing, Innovation, and Corporate Philanthropy, which will be treated in greater detail throughout this book.

Collaboration as a norm

In 2012, an entrepreneur named Eric Migicovsky, having been turned down by several venture capital companies, decided to share his invention with the world and was rewarded with what was, up until recently, the most successful Kickstarter campaign ever, earning over $10 million. Also in 2012, another man appealed to the power of the crowd to raise over $214 million toward his goal. His name was Barack Obama. That same year, the newly inaugurated President of the United States signed into law the JOBS Act, paving the way for companies to raise funds by publicly trading equity without the need for the customary scrutiny, red tape, and regulatory due diligence. This had the crucial effect of allowing entrepreneurs to use crowdfunding platforms to issue private shares of stock to investors. Since then, crowdfunding has grown at an astounding rate— from a handful of online platforms at the end of the last decade, to hundreds of different platforms, catering to almost every possible niche. Together they span a global industry of billions of dollars that has nearly tripled in size in the last two years alone. And, as it continues to grow, so does it evolve.

What began as an alternative mode of finance, a grass-roots movement, is becoming much more. Crowdfunding, at its core, is a method of bringing people together for a common goal. As such, it is a community tool, spreading through established communities but also creating them in its wake. After all, what is a community but a bunch of people who bond over their common interests; and the Internet, in which we live so much of our lives, has provided an influx of new communities. We are no longer limited by borders and geographical distances, and we are barely limited by language and cultural differences.

Crowdfunding platforms have synergized seamlessly with this development. Every forum of environmentalists has become a potential donors' pool for crowdfunded ecological projects, every message board a billboard, and every Facebook group a potential client base. But the opposite is also true. Many crowdfunding projects have also sprouted their own online communities of loyal, active, vocal members.

One of the biggest changes in how we use the Internet has been a shift towards decentralized, peer-to-peer type consumption. This movement, also dubbed the "sharing economy," appears in almost every aspect of our online lives. Where we used to entertain ourselves by watching television or reading a book, we still do, but we also check in on Facebook or watch YouTube and Vine videos. Where once we relied on tabloids and newspapers for information, we still do, but now we also have direct access to millions of sources through collaborative platforms such as Twitter,

Wikipedia, and the *Huffington Post*. Where once we used to buy products from commercial vendors and book hotel rooms from... well, hotels, we still do, but now we also consume these services from private individuals on platforms such as eBay and Airbnb.

One of the main reasons for this is the social development of the Internet. We talk, share, rate, like, and review much more than we used to. It is now more convenient and transparent to purchase a product from a person when their whole history and all of their interactions are laid bare, than it is dealing with a faceless corporation that hides behind commercial secrecy and does its best to avoid scrutiny and oversight. It is also easier to see in real time when your friends are all using a new app or joining a new trend.

But while the sharing economy offers us new sources of entertainment, information, and even chauffeur services, it doesn't cancel out the old ones. No amount of YouTube videos will make television obsolete and eBay is not putting stores out of business. On the contrary, many YouTube videos are excerpts from TV shows, allowing fans to discuss and share favorite moments, thus enhancing the popularity and pop culture relevance of the original show. The same is true for eBay, which many companies now use to sell their goods online, so reducing their overheads and streamlining the whole process. Companies and organizations that adapt to the new reality will find that the sharing economy and new social interactions provide opportunity rather than competition.

Like many innovative concepts, crowdfunding has often

been hailed—and feared—as a disruptive force. Some people have gone so far as to predict that it will come to replace such traditional funding mechanisms as venture capitalists and angel investors. However, as crowdfunding becomes more prevalent, it is increasingly obvious that its force is one of synergy rather than disruption.

The recent rise of crowdfunding, rather than edge out traditional funding sources, seems to have encouraged their growth. In fact they are now enjoying their most prosperous period since the economic recession of the last decade. But this effect is not limited to finance institutions alone. Every user of crowdfunding has discovered that it can augment and bolster many aspects of their activities, by harnessing the core strength of the sharing economy: the crowd asset.

More than a funding mechanism

Crowdfunding is no longer just a means of finance; it is not the disruptive force it has falsely been proclaimed to be and it is not a system to overthrow all other systems. Rather, it is a tool for connecting, for finding shared ideas and shared goals, and for bringing people together. And it is a highly adaptable tool, synergizing with other mechanisms in many different areas.

As a driving force in innovation, crowdfunding has much to offer not just start-ups, but established corporations as well. Crowdfunding can be used to validate and provide proof of concept. It can speed up development by harnessing the collective thoughts and experiences of a large group, refining and improving on existing ideas. It can be used as a tool in selecting investment partners and it can even be employed as an internal mechanism to encourage improvement, entrepreneurship, and innovation from within. Big companies often fear becoming stagnant and losing the ability to compete in an evolving market. But by using crowdfunding creatively, they can promote internal innovation as well as acquire a continuous influx of new ideas while maintaining a connection with their target audience; the main power of crowdfunding is the ability to engage.

As a tool for marketing, crowdfunding is a natural benefactor. Marketing is all about creating and maintaining a connection with customers and potential customers—an intrinsic byproduct of the crowdfunding process. Even crowdfunding campaigns that are strictly focused on fundraising go a long way toward creating an engaged customer base, increasing product and brand awareness, and establishing avenues for future marketing. These effects can be multiplied tenfold when properly applied by an established company. As well as directly funding sales, a crowdfunding tool can be used to leverage marketing efforts and boost sales indirectly by creating product awareness and increasing media impressions and web traffic extraordinarily.

Another area where crowdfunding may have a significant, if indirect, impact on company performance is in the field of public relations. Crowdfunding tools can not only help a company connect better with its community, but also allow the community members to become an actual part of the company's Corporate Social Responsibility plan. When a company and its public work together for a common cause it can have a significant impact, both on the community and on the company's marketability.

Crowdfunding can even be used as a tool to stimulate economic development by providing small businesses with crowd-asset resources, providing supplemental funding, and encouraging and directing other finance mechanisms. Companies and organizations that wish to invest in start-up ventures, whether for profit or non-profit goals, can use crowdfunding tools as a means of validating opportunities and weeding out unripe ones.

An evolution

This is just the beginning. The cases presented in this book are the first steps taken by some of the biggest brand names and organizations on the globe—a foray into a new world of corporate crowdfunding—and many others have begun to follow suit, adapting to an evolving reality. And that's what crowdfunding is—an evolution, not a revolution. It's what's next.

Crowdfunding fosters engagement, active participation, free-market principles, and mutually assured advancement, all while synergizing with current trends of collaborative consumption and social interaction. But the best thing about crowdfunding is that it synergizes with itself. The more crowdfunding there is, the more power it has—just like a speeding object that gains momentum as it grows in mass. We hope this book will both inform and inspire— leading to more involvement in crowdfunding as it exists today and to the creation of new crowdfunding ideas and applications for the benefit of all.

1

A NEW ERA IN CROWDFUNDING

Kevin Berg Grell and Dan Marom

Arguably the most novel funding mechanism to emerge in the past decade, crowdfunding has become one of the most viable methods of sourcing early-stage and seed capital. Its origins lie in the concept of crowdsourcing, where the "crowd" is used to obtain ideas, solutions, and feedback for the development of activities or initiatives. Crowdfunding, in contrast, is described by Wikipedia as the "collective effort of individuals who network and pool their resources, usually via the Internet, to support efforts initiated by other people or organizations."

Most crowdfunding campaigns take place on purpose-designed platforms, most of which require the entrepreneur to meet a certain funding goal within an allotted time-frame; if the designated goal is not pledged by the funders, the funds are returned and the project is cancelled. It is a method used for a limitless range of projects, including, but not limited to, disaster relief, start-up company funding, film-making, gaming, and disease and healthcare research and development.

Whereas traditional funding routes such as bank loans or venture capital center on large dollar investments, crowdfunding solicits small contributions from large numbers of people. Moreover, crowdfunding provides access to the minds of the donors and crowd, allowing businesses and project owners to test and market an idea on a group before bringing it to market. There are several different crowdfunding models that make this possible, which rely on a variety of motivations among donors:

Donation-based
Contributions are given in the form of a donation. Donors are motivated by social or intrinsic aims and do not receive tangible benefits (i.e. no money, equity, or perk) in return. Example: Donately (www. donate.ly)

Peer-to-peer lending
Contributions are given in the form of a loan. Lenders are motivated by a desire for returns on their investment and intrinsic aims, and receive repayment of the loan with interest. Occasionally, if the donor is socially motivated, the loan is repaid without interest. Example: Kiva (www.kiva.org)

Equity-based
Contributions are given in the form of an investment. Investors are motivated by a combination of intrinsic, social, and financial reasons and receive a return on investment over time if the business succeeds. Example: CircleUp (www.circleup.com)

Reward-based
Contributions are given in the form of donation or pre-purchase of a product or service. Donors are motivated by the rewards (perks) and by social aims, and receive the reward or perk as payment. Example: Kickstarter (www.kickstarter.com)

In 2012, projects and businesses raised $2.7 billion through these crowdfunding models. Today there are 450 crowdfunding platforms worldwide, with 191 in the United States, 44 in Britain, and over 100 more in the rest of the Eurozone (growing almost daily). To date, reward-based platforms have proven to be the most popular. The Kickstarter platform alone has featured some 58,038 projects, garnering $1,026,290,122.

Early successes

One of Kickstarter's most notable successes is the "Double Fine Adventure" project. Double Fine is a point-and-click adventure game created by Tim Schafer. While Schafer was a veteran of the prominent media firm LucasArts, adventure games were fairly niche and the founders experienced difficulty securing financing for their new game. In February 2012, Schafer launched a Kickstarter campaign to raise $400,000 for Double Fine, with $100,000 destined for film production and the other $300,000 invested in the game. Using a reward-based model, the campaign offered perks ranging from a special edition version of the game (for $100 donors) to lunch with Tim Schafer and Ron Gilbert plus all the perks offered at every other level (for four backers, pledging $100,000). The latter sold out, and Double Fine raised $3,336,371 from 87,142 donors.

During the development of the game, Shafer's team focused its efforts on brainstorming with their community, soliciting their advice on the concept for the location of the game and ideas for future locations and backdrops. Several of the ideas were developed and illustrated by the team's concept artists. Tim Schafer promised to keep fans updated about the progress and development of Double Fine through social media, and the unbridled enthusiasm of the backers can be viewed on the project's Kickstarter website, where backers still engage in dialogue about the game through their virtual community.

Another notable Kickstarter success is the Pebble Watch, a wristwatch that displays messages from a smart-phone via Bluetooth 4.0. While Pebble Technology founder Eric Migicovsky raised $375,000 through venture capital, the company was unable to secure additional funding and turned to Kickstarter to run a rewards-based crowdfund-ing campaign. Pebble Technology set a goal of $100,000 for a five-week campaign, where individuals who pledged $115 received the first Pebble Watches available to the public. Donors were essentially pre-ordering the watch at a discounted price of $115 rather than waiting for it to become commercially available at the retail price of $150. At the end of the five weeks, the Pebble Watch had raised $10,266,844 from 68,928 people.

The success of these two projects offers important lessons about the non-monetary benefits of crowdfunding: crowd wisdom and feedback. The crowdfunding model creates a platform of communication between the funders and the company, whereby the funders can offer feedback and sug-gestions for the product. Pebble Technology, for example, reacted to funder feedback to make their watch water-resistant—an important feature that came from the virtual community of Pebble donors and potential buyers, rather than Pebble Employees.

Like many founders of early growth companies, Eric Migicovsky was qualified and knowledgeable in his field, experiencing earlier success with an acclaimed Blackberry-compatible smart watch called the inPulse. Nonetheless, his pitch for the Pebble Watch was rejected by venture capitalists and angel investors in Silicon Valley. "I wasn't extremely surprised," said Migicovsky in an interview with the *Los Angeles Times*. "Hardware is much harder to raise money for. We were hoping we could convince some people to our vision, but it didn't work out."

Tim Schafer and Ron Gilbert at Double Fine were even more experienced in the gaming sector; Schafer had a number of successful adventure games under his belt at LucasArts, and Ron Gilbert was dubbed the "unofficial father of the genre" by *Wired* magazine. Yet, both individuals expressed their cynicism with traditional funding mechanisms. "If I were to go to a publisher right now and pitch an adventure game," said Schafer, "they'd laugh in my face." Gilbert agreed: "From first-hand experience, I can tell you that if you even utter the words 'adventure game' in a meeting with a publisher you can just pack up your spiffy concept art and leave. You'd get a better reaction by announcing that you have the plague." With a stigmatized genre and laughable reactions from the industry, turning to friends, family, and fans was the only viable alternative.

What is compelling about both of these stories is that the rejection of funding from traditional mechanisms was by no means a reflection on the experience or quality of either the business idea or the entrepreneurs; it was an issue of perceived risk. One of the strengths of crowdfunding is that it reaches a different kind of donor, whose personal attraction to a project can outweigh any risk. Supporters of the Pebble Watch, for example, considered the watch to be new, cool, and geeky. They also got to own one before the product went to market, and, for many people, the perceived social value of being an "early adopter" is worth the risk of investment. Likewise, many of the supporters of Double Fine were already fans of adventure games, and had an emotional connection with the previous works of Ron Gilbert and Tim Schafer.

The benefits for corporations

The perception of risk has proved to be one of the key drivers in the rise of corporate crowdfunding. Traditional providers of investment such as banks, venture capitalists, and angel investors are tied to inherently risk-averse business models, and the economic volatility of the 2008 financial crisis only made matters worse. As traditional sources of funding dried up, crowdfunding increasingly helped to fill the void. More significantly, the use of crowdfunding expanded beyond early-stage companies and first-time entrepreneurs.

Large corporations and enterprises began to experiment with the crowdfunding model as a means of staying afloat in the new economy. What they discovered has led to a fundamental reassessment of who investors are and what they can offer. By expanding the definition of "investor" to include members of the crowd, large enterprises have not only found a new source of funding, they have tapped into an engaged community capable of supplying indispensable resources such as product feedback, market validation, intrapreneurship, and new business models.

Corporations have also discovered that the relationship between business and crowd can be very different to that between business and venture capitalist. In many cases, funding from the crowd is non-dilutive, allowing the organization to retain creative control over the product and service. While they have the option to follow recommendations given by of the thousands of donors who make up the crowd, they are not accountable to them in the same way that they would be to a single venture capitalist firm.

Warner Bros.

A billion-dollar multi-media company does not seem a likely candidate for crowdfunding, but Warner Bros. is partially responsible for the most successful crowdfunding film venture ever undertaken. *Veronica Mars* was a deeply beloved television show that was cancelled after three seasons, without any resolution of the fate of its characters. The series creator, Rob Thomas, was convinced that he had a fan base hungry for more content, but for years Warner Bros., who owns the rights to the series, refused to finance a film. Eventually Thomas and the company came to an agreement. Thomas would use a Kickstarter campaign to raise the necessary funds, which would be deposited into a production account set up by the movie studio. In return,

Warner Bros. agreed to absorb the costs for marketing and film release.

The results were staggering. The *Veronica Mars* campaign raised $5,702,153 from 91,585 individual donors. For Rob Thomas and the *Veronica Mars* team, the payoff was clear: their project was funded. For Warner Bros., the benefits were more nuanced; $5.7 million is not a significant sum of money for a company with such deep pockets. The more significant benefit lay in the market testing and validation. Over 91,000 individuals contributed to the *Veronica Mars* project, underscoring not only the sheer number of potential consumers, but also the number willing to spend their money and time on a project with which they have an emotional connection.

Universal Music Group

Like Warner Bros., Universal Music Group does not seem a natural fit for launching a crowdfunding project. Yet the music group has gone one step further by announcing its own crowdfunding platform called "The Vinyl Project." According to UVinyl, the branch of Universal responsible for vinyl records, the new platform will be: "A crowdfunded vinyl service that makes use of Universal Music's extensive catalogue to offer sought-after deleted records to be re-pressed in this great format. Funders will become owners of limited edition records, which will also include digital downloads & personalized art prints."

Like the *Veronica Mars* film, The Vinyl Project is not expected to post blockbuster profits. While films like *Harry*

Potter and the Deathly Hallows – Part 2 can make over a billion dollars at the box office, smaller films like *Veronica Mars* are not expected to garner such sales. Similarly, in 2012, vinyl accounted for only 1.4 percent of album sales. While that may seem exceedingly small, vinyl sales were up 18 percent from the year before, according to Nielsen. With this in mind, it is critical to note that crowdfunding, besides being a mechanism to absorb the cost of production, is a means of testing the market to assess whether or not a product or service will succeed. For the Universal Music Group, selling 4.6 million physical albums, paired with the 18 percent upswing from the year before, indicates that a sufficiently healthy vinyl market exists.

By bringing crowdfunding into the mix, Universal will be able to secure funding for the production of its out-of-print records, but it will also be able to gauge which albums are most likely to sell to their target market through crowd feedback, ultimately narrowing the risk margin and allowing the organization to deliver exactly the type of product their target market is after.

Procter & Gamble

While Universal Music Group and Warner Bros. are using their existing product portfolio for crowdfunded projects, Procter & Gamble (P&G) is using crowdfunding as a vehicle for scouting new products. The company has partnered with CircleUp, a leading crowdfunding platform that connects new consumer brands with investors. The terms of the partnership mean that P&G has privileged access to CircleUp's portfolio of start-ups, giving it the opportunity to invest in or acquire businesses of interest.

For P&G, much of the appeal lies in the vetting of the consumer brands for market viability. As Andrew Backs, manager of new business creation at P&G, puts it: "If it's a bad idea, then it's just simply not going to get funded." However, the partnership also represents the enterprise's latest step in an evolving approach to innovation.

Henry Chesbrough rightly asserts that the twentieth century was defined by closed innovation, whereby enterprises like P&G innovated internally through large research and development (R&D) budgets and by hiring the smartest people, they could get their hands on. These factors allowed large organizations to get their products to market faster; and once the profits were streaming in, they could be reinvested into R&D and the cycle would start all over again.

Yet the end of the century saw a shift away from this pattern. An increase in mobile workers and knowledge workers twinned with a rise in the use of venture capital led to start-up companies being responsible for many of the breakthrough innovations in the market. Large enterprises like P&G no longer had the monopoly on innovation. They could no longer expect to attract the brightest individuals; instead, those same individuals were turning to venture capitalists to fund their ideas.

P&G needed to find a new way to access bright minds and the answer initially lay in crowdsourcing. Following a change in company leadership in 2000, P&G set an ambitious goal of taking 50 percent of its ideas for growth from outside sources over the next five years. At the time, P&G had about 8,200 staff in its innovation team. Of those, 7,500 were internal team members, 400 were working through P&G suppliers, and 300 were external. Since then P&G has almost doubled the size of the team. According to Larry Huston, the R&D executive who oversaw the transformation: "We still have 7,500 internally but now we have 2,000 with suppliers and 7,000 virtual and extended partners."

P&G's use of crowdsourcing has proved to be an unequivocal success, and the move into crowdfunding via CircleUp is the next step in a fundamental shift towards a more unconventional modus operandi. The benefits are similar: P&G gets access to innovative ideas but it also gains market validation—the individuals providing the feedback or the "wisdom" are the ones actually funding the project itself. These donors have a stake in the success of the product monetarily, yet they are still engaged members of the community and are able to provide not only feedback about the new product or service, but validation of the market. If co-investment is needed by the donors and the enterprise to get the product to market itself, as was the case with Warner Bros. and *Veronica Mars*, the level of risk for the enterprise is reduced because the donors are the potential buyers.

Intrapreneurship

Internal crowdfunding occurs when an enterprise sets up a crowdfunding platform within the boundaries of its own organization in the hopes of expanding its innovation pipeline. It is another dynamic way for enterprises to harness the wisdom of the crowd for the sake of their own products and services. This concept is linked to "intrapreneurship," where companies work to encourage an entrepreneurial attitude among their employees with the end goal of expanding their R&D portfolios. Over the past few years, large enterprises have used the principles of crowdsourcing as a means to achieve "intrapreneurship," designing programs where employees can come together to brainstorm new ideas which are then pitched to the higher-ups within the organization.

Google and Facebook, for example, regularly organize "hackathons" where their software engineers, graphic designers, and interface designers come together for collaboration on software projects. Hackathons are also increasingly popular for enhancing the API or "application program interface." Notably, in 2011, the website Foursquare held a global hackathon in which 500 software developers from thirty countries competed to create new applications using the Foursquare API. The initiative was so successful that Foursquare organized a subsequent hackathon in 2013.

Internal crowdfunding takes the principles of ideation and production innovation from intrapreneurship but extends the concept to include funding. One of the best examples comes from IBM, which has experimented with the model in three of its offices (see page 124 for more details). In the first initiative, in 2012, 500 IBM employees were given $100 each, which they could choose to invest in a project via a specially created internal crowdfunding platform. There were forty projects in total, all proposed by the participants themselves. The only rules were that participants were not allowed to allocate their $100 to their own projects, and if they chose not to spend the money at all, they would lose it.

A variety of projects were proposed and funded, ranging from purchasing a 3D printer for office use to hosting a lecture series. The team behind the 3D printer found clever ways of pitching their project to other employees, such as posting a sign next to the office printer that said "Don't You Wish You Were Printing on a 3D Printer Right Now?" Another project proposed that social robots be purchased to represent team members who worked remotely. To inspire participants to fund their idea, the team borrowed one such social robot and sent it zooming around the offices and corridors as a social representation of the employee. Both the 3D printer and the company social robot were funded.

While the scope of these projects was very much limited to meeting cultural and technical challenges within the organization, other enterprises have used innovative combinations of internal and external crowdfunding to broader effect.

Local Motors

John B. Rogers was serving in the United States Marine Corps when he came up with the idea of Local Motors. Like his predecessors at Tesla and Better Place, Rogers wanted to bring environmentally conscious cars to market. By focusing on design and production efficiency, Rogers wanted to make it possible for his buyers to be participants in the manufacturing process, a type of business model that would prevent unbought cars from rusting over in dealership parking lots.

Rogers channelled his vision into what is now known as Local Motors, the world's first open-source car company. The company brings together a global community of designers, engineers, fabricators and car enthusiasts to bring new automobiles to market through distributed manufacturing channels. Local Motors also has partnerships in place with large enterprises including Siemens, Shell, and BMW. As part of their partnership with Siemens, for example, Local Motors gains access to computer-aided design (CAD) software, which it then recommends to its global community of 30,000 designers.

Local Motors also works with large enterprises through hosted challenges, whereby the enterprise may outsource a design task to the Local Motors community of designers in exchange for cash prizes. For example, in 2012, the BMW Group challenged the community to define the future "premium vehicle" in exchange for a cash prize. The parameters required the designers to address issues such as interior design, connectivity, and functionality.

In early December 2013, Local Motors launched its first crowdfunding campaign. In partnership with the San Francisco-based crowdfunding platform Crowdtilt (now Tilt), the campaign aims to raise funding for "The Cruiser"—a stylish motorized bicycle designed by Ianis Vasilatos, a longtime Local Motors community member. Vasilatos designed The Cruiser in response to a posted challenge in the Local

Motors community and his design was selected over 100 others. The campaign aims to raise $50,000 to finish the development of the bicycle and bring it to market.

According to Local Motors Chief Strategy Officer Justin Fishkin, "the addition of crowdfunding to our existing co-creation, micro-manufacturing, and retail capabilities completes the tool set used by our global community to bring the most innovative vehicular products to market." While this is its first crowdfunding project, Local Motors plans to use the model to fund many of the projects or ideas that come from its extensive user base.

As Jay Rogers, Chief Executive Officer of Local Motors explains, the company expects to realize significant advantages: "By integrating crowdfunding capabilities into our platform we will empower our community to deliver a world of vehicle innovations—from full vehicles and portable electric chargers to specialty automotive components—an accelerated pace not possible through traditional vehicle design, development, and funding methods."

Amazon

Retail giant Amazon recently dipped into the crowdfunding world with the launch of its program "Amazon Birthday Gift." Through Facebook, individuals can call on members of their social network to donate a small number of dollars towards an Amazon Gift Card for a mutual friend's birthday gift. The program, which encourages customers to "Use your social network to spread some love," is Amazon's first crowdfunding initiative and it remains to be seen whether or not the company will expand the initiative to allow patrons to crowdfund other products sold on their website.

Chrysler

Car manufacturer Chrysler has also experimented with crowdfunding, offering customers the ability to enlist the help of family and friends to purchase the 2013 Dodge Dart (see page 41 for more details). Working like a wedding registry, DodgeDartRegistry.com lists the different components of the car separately on a website and offers them up for individual purchase. The components range in price according to how much donors can afford to spend. The Dart, which has a starting price of $15,995, is well suited to the project. It is very much designed for social media-savvy millennials, who may not be able to afford the car themselves, but who can promote a crowdfunding campaign through Facebook, Twitter, and other social media outlets. This then allows customers to create a larger "virtual community" of family and friends who might want to contribute to the purchase of the car as part of a graduation gift or birthday present.

The Dodge Dart program has not adopted the "all or nothing" model of Kickstarter.com; the funding goal can be for any amount of money and the registrant can select a campaign length of thirty, sixty or ninety days. After the campaign is over, Dodge mails the registrant a check, which they can use any way they want. According to one such registrant from DodgeDartRegistry.com, "I have had the same car since I graduated high school and I need a new one for my sons and I. Hopefully 2013 will be the year we get one." Her goal is to raise $23,000 for a Dodge Dart in the vivid color of True Blue Pearl and she no doubt told as many people as possible about it. For the Chrysler Group, of course, any mention of the campaign via social media channels is a form of free advertising and a means of breaking into the competitive millennial car market that has traditionally been dominated by the Honda Civic.

Summary

One thing that the examples in this chapter demonstrate is that crowdfunding is not a replacement for traditional methods of securing investment; it is an additional new tool for corporations to employ. For example, if the average cost for drug development costs $2 billion, crowdfunding alone is not the answer; but it can be used strategically by a pharmaceutical company as part of the support needed for the full lifecycle of product development. This is important for two reasons: first, the financial risk and burden is spread among a combination of financial supporters or investors, rather than relying on one such mechanism; second, utilizing more than one mechanism allows the enterprise company to have access to a "super crowd" of venture capitalists, partners, customers and all stakeholders who have a desire to see a certain product or service come to fruition. For the enterprise, using the crowd's affinity groups, prediction markets, price discovery, risk sharing, and social networking is a very efficient early-phase funding mechanism, and is a cost-effective way to source great investment opportunities.

But what these examples demonstrate above all is that crowdfunding is much more than a mere financing mechanism. If used correctly, crowdfunding is a dynamic concept that can provide established, capable businesses with a huge competitive advantage, most notably in the fields of marketing, innovation and corporate social responsibility. Over the course of the next three chapters, we will explore each of these fields in turn, assessing the most recent developments and identifying some emerging trends. We will present case studies based on our own research, and we will showcase "insider views" written exclusively for this book by key first-movers and other experts in the field. We will then present a final section exploring some of the more far-reaching implications of crowdfunding principles. First, though, let's take a look at what crowdfunding can offer the world of marketing.

2

CROWDFUNDING AND MARKETING

Kevin Berg Grell and Dan Marom

In its strictest sense, crowdfunding refers to the mechanism by which a product is financed and brought into being. Traditionally this process occurs before a product is brought to market and is therefore outside the scope of the client-product relationship. However, in crowdfunding, the boundaries between financing, product development, and marketing are more blurred because the financiers are often the clients as well and are funding the venture by pre-purchasing the product. In essence, the product is brought to market in order to finance its development and production. It is important to understand the difference between usual pre-selling and crowdfunding in this context. When companies pre-sell, they do so after the decision to go into production is taken, but the retail price is still uncertain; the public is in this sense surveyed for information that guides the pricing decision. With crowdfunding, companies are sourcing similar information, but at a much earlier point in time. This difference—and the blurring of disciplinary boundaries in general—also means that there are ways to harness the power of the crowd to give a boost to the marketing process itself.

Market validation

Whether you are an aspiring entrepreneur or a multinational corporation, developing and mass-producing a new product requires enormous investment. New businesses often have to convince outside parties that their products are worth investing in, but even large, well-established firms seek to minimize the chances of failure by trying to predict how the market will react to their new product: movie studios hold screenings before a movie is released, in order to gauge the reaction of potential movie-goers; other industries employ beta testing, focus groups, polls, analysts, and statisticians in order to try and determine whether a product will be successful. In the world of crowdfunding, market validation of this kind is an integral component of the process. This does not mean that crowdfunded products cannot fail, but it does allow companies to mitigate against the consequences of these failures.

As we have already established, a crowdfunded product is generally brought to market *in order* to be financed and brought into being. To ensure that result, the product must exhibit a measure of success on the market. This means that the risks and costs associated with the development of that new product are only undertaken if the product has succeeded to the point of nullifying those risks and mitigating at least part of those costs.

Take, for example, those products sold under the label of LEGO Ideas (formerly LEGO CUUSOO). The company has created a platform by which customers design their own LEGO product and offer it up to other customers. If a design reaches 10,000 supporters it becomes a candidate for production and retail. Not only are LEGO using their customers to help design and market the products for them; they are ensuring that there is a market for their products before they go into production.

The financial benefits of this approach are clear, but LEGO Ideas also demonstrates one of the greatest advantages of this kind of "sharing economy": the reduction, if not elimination, of waste. While companies can assuredly find ways of being successful and profitable without the added benefits of crowdfunding, there will always be failures and mistakes made along the way. This is not necessarily a bad thing. Mistakes and failures help us to learn and grow. But the cost of these mistakes can have a negative impact on everyone associated with them. A failed venture can cause a company and its shareholders financial loss; it can lead to redundancies to improve efficiency; and it can even affect customers if the company can only remain viable by rolling the cost of the failure into the prices of its other products.

This is why the cost reduction benefits of crowdfunding are so significant. Just as a plant will thrive and flourish if you cut off sick branches and trim back unnecessary off-shoots, so will a market that is not bogged down by the cost of failures.

Finding a market for the product

Sometimes products are developed to answer the needs of a particular community or subset of customers. This is often true of established companies with an existing client base. In these situations the marketing process is about identifying the need and suggesting a product to meet it.

However, many times it is the reverse. A company dedicated to research and development, intent on innovation and not becoming stagnant, will come up with a new product or idea for a product. One of the first steps of the marketing process is then finding a market for the product, or establishing whether there is one at all.

To this end companies try to identify likely customers for their product by looking at people who purchased similar products, or whose habits and lifestyles would likely benefit from the use of the product. But reaching those people can be difficult given that so many of us are jaded by constant and increasingly aggressive advertising (it is no surprise that some of the most popular inventions are those that help us avoid the constant harassment of marketing, such as TiVo, Netflix, and even browser extensions like Adblock).

What if there were a venue for new products where people were, if not avid enthusiasts, then at least interested parties, ready to listen? What if there were hundreds of these venues, catering to almost every possible interest, from biotechnology to gourmet cuisine? What if the people who inhabited these marketing microcosms were not just likely customers, but also potential messengers willing to spread the gospel of an exciting new gadget or an upcoming trend? Wouldn't an intelligent marketer jump at the chance to take advantage of these venues and sounding boards?

In 2012 it was estimated that there were over 500 active crowdfunding platforms which, according to industry reports, raised over $2.7 billion in financing. In 2013 that number almost doubled to $5.1 billion, with even greater growth anticipated in 2014. Some of these platforms include a broad variety of projects and some were created for more specialized niches. But one thing that they all have in common is that their users are willing browsers and shoppers. They flip through different products and listen to the pitches made by their developers, because they want to.

By launching a product on a crowdfunding platform a company ensures that it will be seen and evaluated by a community of keen, open-minded people. And if a project is well received, such success can help a company identify the market for the product and help to grow it. Take ConsumerPhysics, a company that launched a highly portable molecular sensor product called SCiO via a Kickstarter campaign. The campaign helped to finance development of the product while also identifying a target audience, and the product's backers and supporters used their own networks to further grow that market.

Expanding the market in this way was also one of the side benefits of the Dodge Dart Register program launched by Chrysler (see page 41). This program allowed customers to register the car they wish to own and invite friends and family members to fund its purchase piece by piece. Dodge therefore got to sell cars to customers who otherwise couldn't afford one, but the marketing mechanism also connected the company to the many people who acted as funders. These weren't strangers buying random pieces of machinery; they were a community of people with a common goal. And, crucially, they represented a new pool of potential customers.

Customer engagement

Large corporations and organizations regularly donate to their local communities, whether by funding their own community service programs or by giving to particular charities. In today's age of global awareness and widespread availability of information, it is almost a requirement for companies to be seen giving back to the public. This is a topic that we explore in detail in Chapter 4 (see page 137). However, while companies may be quick to burnish their charitable credentials, we must bear in mind that this too forms part of the client-product relationship and so falls under the scope of marketing.

One of the hottest topics in today's marketing world is that of customer engagement. Studies show that companies that engage their customers are more than twice as likely to succeed as those that do not. In this context, and considering that donations and charity costs are factored into the cost of doing business, companies can benefit from allowing their customers a more direct influence over their charitable activities.

When a customer purchases a product, a portion of the purchase price may go towards funding the company's charitable activities. This is a given. However, consider the mechanism used by Waitrose, a supermarket chain in the United Kingdom. The company's "Community Matters" scheme operates under the pledge: "We support good causes. You decide who gets what." Every time a customer completes a shopping visit, they are presented with a token, which they can place in one of three boxes prominently displayed near the shop's entrance. Each box represents a charity local to that branch. At the end of every month, each branch of Waitrose then donates a total of £1,000 ($1,600) to the three charities, but the way the sum is divided up depends on how many tokens each cause gets. The same scheme is also provided online, but with a monthly sum of £25,000 ($39,000) divided between three national causes voted for by customers once they complete the online checkout process. Through this creative use of their crowd-asset—and at no extra cost—Waitrose is gaining the customer's good will, engagement, and emotional investment every time they make a purchase.

Another example more directly associated with marketing would be the crowdsourcing of a company's advertising activities—one of the most essential and expensive items on a marketing budget. Companies spend fortunes on premium commercial spots (a one-minute television ad spot during the Super Bowl can cost as much as $9 million) and even larger amounts on producing the funniest, cleverest, most original material in the hopes of grabbing as much public awareness as they can.

This has only been exacerbated by the advent of the Internet. Over the last decade and a half the word viral has come to signify the spreading of information and ideas through YouTube clips, Vines, and memes, more than the spreading of infectious diseases. One of the biggest challenges for advertising firms in recent years has been duplicating the success spontaneously achieved by amateur videos such as "Charlie bit my finger" and "Harlem Shake," as well as countless flashmobs, marriage proposals, and laughing babies.

One of the most widely spread viral campaigns in recent months was the Ice Bucket Challenge to promote awareness of Amyotrophic Lateral Sclerosis or ALS. This campaign, purportedly initiated by a person with ALS rather than some clever marketing firm, reached a climax during the summer of 2014. Millions of people took part in the challenge, which involved pouring a bucket of ice water over their heads, posting a video of it online, and then nominating friends to do the same. Some did not go on to make the final step, which was to make a donation to ALS, and others may not even have realised that ALS was involved, but the success of the campaign cannot be doubted. Public awareness of ALS skyrocketed, fuelled by social media, and the ALS Association raised over $100 million in one month, more than quintupling the total raised in the entire previous year.

From a marketing perspective though, perhaps the most interesting fact about the ALS campaign was the number of different videos created and shared during its course. According to the *New York Times*, more than 1.2 million videos of the challenge were shared on Facebook between June and August of 2014. This wasn't just a case of a *particular* viral video being shared millions of times. These were a million *different* videos being shared. Why is this so interesting?

Approximately 90 million people tune in each year to watch the Super Bowl (the holy grail of advertising opportunities). We've already established that an advertising spot during the game can cost several million dollars, not to mention the cost of producing it, which can also range in the millions. All told, advertisers who take this one-off spot, which only comes round once a year, have to budget in excess of $1 for every ten people the ad reaches.

Now let's take a look at how YouTube works. YouTube

actively encourages people to post videos by offering them financial rewards based on the number of people who watch the video. There are various elements to factor in but for the sake of simplification, we can say that Google pays its YouTube partners $1 for every 1,000 people who watch the video. For the average person this isn't exactly a gold mine. But there is a growing number of people who have focused their careers on making YouTube videos, and who are making a decent living doing so. In fact, according to some accounts, the top twenty YouTubers could be making over $1 million a year from ad revenues alone.

What does this have to do with crowdfunding? On the one hand we have a community of people who are very good at making viral YouTube videos and are doing so for as little as $1 per 1,000 views, and on the other we have companies willing to pay up to $100 per 1,000 views for their ads. This situation spells opportunity for the crowd-empowered marketer.

For instance, why not launch a creative, original campaign, allowing YouTube users to make their own ads for a product, and paying them a tenth of what it costs to reach the same number of people through conventional means? Not only are you creating a campaign that has the potential to reach far more people while saving on the cost of doing so; you are also leveraging crowdsourcing in the actual production of the ads.

Crowdfunding doesn't just have potential benefits for entrepreneurs or large corporations; it has much to offer non-profits, universities, and even municipalities and governments. The same principles that apply to profit-oriented companies can be adapted to benefit any organization that relies on interaction with the public. And the possibilities are endless. The examples that follow show how crowdfunding is being used in different corporations from a marketing perspective. Some are case studies based on our own research; others are insider views written by people who have put crowdfunding to use in their own organizations. All of them offer valuable insights.

CHRYSLER

Dan Marom and Kevin Berg Grell

After its launch in July 2012, Chrysler's new Dodge Dart sold only 25,303 cars in the remainder of that year. In stark contrast, competing models such as the Honda Civic, Toyota Corolla, and Chevrolet Cruze all topped sales numbers of 200,000 (the Civic taking top honors with over 317,000).

Chrysler CEO Sergio Marchionne said that sales of the Dodge Dart may have been affected by the sense that it was underpowered, but he later called the car "perfect," adding that it could and would do better.

On January 20, the following year, Dodge duly launched a campaign aimed at boosting sales of its new 2013 Dart. It comprised a thirty second video on "how to change buying cars forever." According to its own video, the concept for the campaign was modeled on a bridal registry, which also gave the campaign its name: the Dodge Dart Registry.

The idea is simple. Let people register for a new Dodge Dart, and their friends and family will co-fund the car by each sponsoring a different component. A carefully designed website enables backers to literally see which part of the car they are backing; it also offers ways to customize the car, with a choice of twelve exterior colors and numerous interior and under-the-hood options. Once a car is registered on the website, the person registering it (who has to be over eighteen and a United States resident) has the option to share the registry on Facebook and Twitter. They must also set a specific goal and time limit for the registry, of up to ninety days. When the car is fully funded, the registrant can then pick up his or her brand new Dodge Dart at the dealership. "The registry is designed to make the process of configuring and buying a new Dart more social than ever," said Olivier François, Chrysler's Chief Marketing Officer.

The first car to be purchased through the scheme was funded under the title "Toni's Registry," by the parish of Northstar Church in Clifton Park, NY. The registry was set up by a friend for a woman who needed the car in order to make long, weekly trips for medical treatments. Her community answered the call, raising over $22,600 in twenty-one days. In addition to presenting the surprised woman with a brand new car (she had only learned about the registry a few days prior to the presentation), Dodge also gave her a $2,000 gift card for purchasing gas, and announced a $20,000 donation to the Triple Negative Breast Cancer Foundation.

Dodge quickly shifted its marketing messaging in reaction to the large number of campaigns being created by community and not-for-profit organizations. The extremely positive online sentiment experienced by Dodge during this campaign in part is due to the influence of these community organizations. One can argue that without this strong social connection, the online community might have reacted negatively to the campaign; instead the sentiment was exceptionally positive.

Campaign results
In terms of number of cars funded through the campaign's

website, the Dodge Dart Registry was not a resounding success. Less than forty were directly sold through the site. Of those who did not manage to get their registered cars funded, few even got close, with hundreds of thousands of components remaining unfunded.

However, the campaign helped reach tens of thousands of potential new customers and boosted the car's sales to more than double in the following quarter, leading Dodge to hail it a marketing success. According to Melissa Garlick, head of Dodge brand advertising, the campaign generated more than 70 million media impressions, over 840,000 unique page views, and an average time spent on the website of about 11 minutes. The two fully funded cars, she says, were just "a nice cherry on top" (the remaining cars sold via the Dodge Registry were partially funded by the crowd and by the campaign creators themselves).

The wider effects of the campaign may not have been limited to the Dodge brand name, or even the Chrysler Group, though. A similar campaign was launched by Hyundai with very different results, which could signify a change in how cars are sold in future. Hyundai launched its own crowdfunding campaign by partnering with online platform, Motozuma.com. The campaign sold about 1,600 cars out of over 700,000; or approximately 0.25 percent of the cars sold by Hyundai in the U.S. According to Nathan Miller, senior group manager of incentives for Hyundai Motor America, this method of purchasing a car appeals to younger consumers and first-time buyers, stating that 64 percent of customers who bought a new Hyundai with the aid of the Motozuma website were thirty-five or younger. "That is a demographic that every automotive manufacturer is after," Miller points out.

Differences between the Dodge Dart and Hyundai campaigns may help explain the disparate results. While Dodge used their own domain name, Hyundai sat alongside the rest of the Motozuma.com partners on its website; Dodge only applied the offer to the Dart, whereas Hyundai did not limit their campaign to a single car or model; Dodge required that the car be fully funded in order to purchase, while Hyundai used their campaign to help people afford a down payment on a car; and Dodge did not offer any sort of monetary incentive upfront, whereas Hyundai openly advertised that they would match contributions dollar for dollar up to $500.

Conclusion

The Dodge Dart Registry did not net many sales directly, but that wasn't wholly unexpected. For the company's marketing team, the fundraising aspect of the campaign was incidental to its other benefits.

First of all, the Registry created a great deal of awareness, engagement, and word-of-mouth advertising—all of it positive. This was especially evident in the way that the offer was taken up by community organizations and causes, who acted as effective brand evangelists. Second, the registrants made active use of social media channels to promote their individual campaigns. Car firms have long wanted to use such channels as direct sales tools but have struggled to do so; crowdfunding might take them a step closer. Thirdly, as the Hyundai campaign demonstrated, crowdfunding appeals to a younger demographic—one that every car firm is competing to reach. This may simply be a function of the relative novelty of the crowdfunding mechanism itself—perhaps the demographic base will widen as awareness of crowdfunding grows—but for now it represents a new avenue to extend a company's marketing reach.

YOUTUBE

Josef Holm, Tubestart

A year ago, if an indie rock band wanted to record a new CD but didn't have the money, it might have turned to crowd-funding. It would have used a platform such as Kickstarter to launch their funding campaign, and then conjured up a variety of creative rewards for the fans who donated funds (signed copies of their CD for $40, a specially written song for $200, the lead singer shaving his head on stage for $500). They would probably have launched their campaign at a live show, and then blasted links out to all of their fans through Facebook, Twitter, Google+, and YouTube for four weeks. Those fans that wished to contribute to the band would have had to leave the site on which they follow their band and go to Kickstarter to donate. And at the end of the four weeks, if the band met or exceeded its preset financial target, it would get to keep the money and download it to their PayPal account. If it failed, it would get nothing.

Today, that same band can conduct an almost *perpetual* crowdfunding campaign through YouTube and reach more viewers than every other crowdfunding and microlending site combined. Instead of preparing an elaborate, time-bound fundraising campaign involving multiple sites, bands can campaign and receive payment through a single crowd-funding portal. They can also organically and continuously solicit donations while building their fan base, enabling them to enjoy spikes in donations after each concert they play, and to expand their audience at every new city they visit. They can choose to reward fans (or not) because the contributions are donation-based rather than rewards-based. Perhaps most importantly, fans don't need to toggle between multiple sites in order to enjoy their music and also support their band.

YouTube and Fan-Funding

YouTube is one of the biggest websites in the world. More than a billion monthly viewers use it to watch an astonishing more than 6 billion hours of online video, taking advantage of a search engine second in size only to YouTube's parent company Google.com. And this incredibly large user base enjoys access to an almost limitless variety of new content, which is provided willingly, *for free*, by individuals around the world. It is one of the largest and most engaged social media networks on the Internet, making it uniquely well positioned to tap into the crowdfunding market.

The site's first move into the field came in June 2014 with the launch of its "Fan Funding" feature—an embedded "tip jar" payment mechanism that enables video creators to ask their fans for one-time payments in support of their work. The feature is currently only available in the U.S., Australia, Japan, and Mexico, but it is likely to become available soon to the other sixty-one markets that YouTube is localized for and in which Google Wallets operates. In fact, once Fan Funding is enabled for the majority of the site's creators, YouTube will boast by far the biggest crowdfunding platform in the world as far as audience reach is concerned.

With this vast potential in mind, YouTube stands to reap tremendous gains. Foremost is the opening of a significant new revenue stream. Since its launch in 2005, YouTube has experimented with different ways of monetizing its service, as well as entering other markets with established revenue streams. It started life as a simple video-sharing site for accessing footage that individuals may have missed in the news or videos that they wanted to share among friends. Famously, the first video was simply a short piece showing one of the founders, Jawed Karim at the San Diego Zoo.

Within a year the company's growth dwarfed all expectations. It received approximately 65,000 uploads and over 100 million views per day. This volume attracted the attention of NBC who developed an advertising partnership with YouTube in early 2006, a partnership that may be considered YouTube's first true revenue stream. It also led to Google's acquisition of the site later that same year.

Although YouTube has recently introduced a subscription-based service offering a limited number of channels for a monthly fee, advertising remains the site's most steadfast revenue generator. Initially built from a short-lived partnership with AdSense in 2007, YouTube established an advertising revenue sharing arrangement with video providers (consisting of a 45/55 split between YouTube and the uploader). The model not only ensures that

YouTube gains revenue; it also drives users to contribute more content and continuously build viewership.

Yet despite the critical role of advertising, advertising *rates* have been threatened in recent years as the number of videos available continues to exceed the number of ads (rates are typically based upon CPM or clicks per thousand views and those views become more difficult to acquire as the volume of videos increases). As a result users of YouTube looking to fund their creative contributions and videos through advertising face an increasingly dire picture. In addition, YouTube faces growing competition from web streaming services such as Netflix, which is free of advertisements. Therefore, while everyday users of the site may prefer to support their work through traditional advertising, they would likely enjoy the complementary capacity of accepting (or even soliciting) donations from their fan base.

In this sense, YouTube's Fan Funding feature is a natural extension to its prior monetization efforts. It is a means for collecting funds from fans in a manner that is aligned with, and indeed driven by the desire of YouTube contributors to draw revenue from their own creations. In short, YouTube has found another way to inspire YouTube viewers and producers to continually produce content, while simply taking a cut of the transaction.

However, Fan Funding is more than just a revenue enhancer for users of YouTube; it also represents a more fundamental shift by the site into the arena of crowdfunding. YouTube has long been used as an extension of crowdfunding campaigns. When someone creates a campaign on Kickstarter, for example, they typically promote it via YouTube as well as other social media channels such as Facebook, Twitter, and LinkedIn. The most commonly used method for a user to do this is to embed a link on their YouTube site, a link that takes potential donors away from YouTube and brings them over to Kickstarter (or Indiegogo, Tubestart, etc.) where they can then view the full campaign and contribute funds. There were two main drawbacks to this from YouTube's perspective. Not only were crowdfunding campaigns drawing eyes away from their site, they were driving them away to other sites on which the viewers were likely to donate or contribute funds online. This presented a two-fold financial problem. First, turning viewers away from YouTube threatened its advertising revenue. Second, YouTube viewers were contributing funds elsewhere, and other platforms were reaping the profits.

Fan Funding was ostensibly introduced to address both of these issues. Potential donors can now contribute money without clicking away from YouTube, thus securing its advertising revenues and opening a new channel for revenue. This seemingly innocuous change may not only provide YouTube with a new source of revenue but might also enable it to change the manner in which individuals conceive of crowdfunding.

YouTube's advantages

YouTube's Fan Funding feature is a type of donation-based crowdfunding—a much simpler mechanism than found on rewards-based platforms such as Indiegogo and equity-based platforms such as CrowdCube. Specifically, those who fundraise on YouTube do not have to establish a preset deadline for their campaign (nor do they even have to establish a "campaign" at all). This enables individuals to raise funds continuously. YouTube also does not require a specific fundraising target, and therefore the fundraisers not only get to keep all of their funds, but are free from strict notions of "success" or "failure" as defined by their fundraising platform.

In addition, YouTube fundraisers are not required to develop a set of rewards for donors, nor do they have to establish a separate campaign page (or even a business plan, as is the case with some equity-based sites). Fans on YouTube can simply make a one-time financial contribution to a channel without a specific crowdfunding goal and without any expectations of reciprocity.

Furthermore, while it is not currently possible for YouTube fundraisers to set up monthly recurring subscription payments from their fans, this does appear to be a natural next step in the process, and a step that would further differentiate it from its crowdfunding competitors (Tubestart is the only platform currently offering perpetual subscription crowdfunding campaigns).

In addition to providing fundraisers with a simpler platform, YouTube also offers users its extraordinary reach, its monthly 1 billion viewers easily eclipsing the traffic of any competitor crowdfunding site. Of course, it must be noted that only a fraction of those billion viewers currently choose YouTube with the intention of donating money, but this perception may change as users gradually become more aware of the feature. And, regardless, the number of eyes on the site remains a clear competitive advantage.

YouTube holds a competitive position on price as well. Fan Funding contributions are processed through the Google Wallet payment system at a comparatively low rate of 5 percent plus $0.21 per transaction. By contrast, Kickstarter charges a fee of 5 percent of funds raised, plus payment or processing fees that range from 3–5 percent. Indiegogo charges between 4 percent and 9 percent of the raised funds, in addition to approximately 3 percent processing fees. In fact the most cost effective alternative to Fan Funding is for YouTubers to place a link to PayPal on their site, which costs $0.30 per donation plus 2.9 percent.

In short, YouTube possesses all the ingredients for a seamless and successful crowdfunding platform. It has copious amounts of traffic (an exceptional crowd) who watch an incredible volume of video (exceptional engagement). It also boasts a competitive price advantage and a fully integrated payment processing system that enables users to contribute money without leaving the Google ecosystem. The only requirement for participation in Fan Funding is a verified YouTube partner account in good standing and a Google Wallet account. Once a YouTube account is connected with Google Wallet and a bank account is connected users can enable Fan Funding on any or all of their videos and collect contributions perpetually. This greatly simplified process, added to the power of YouTube's scope and the cost advantage all point to a successful future for YouTube in the field of crowdfunding.

YouTube's disadvantages

In spite of YouTube's potential, it remains to be seen whether or not its tip jar model will become a widely adopted success story or a novelty; it has just hit the market so there is no hard data to back any projected performance analytics. However, it is worth noting a few potential drawbacks that may hinder its performance.

From the users' perspective, there are few downsides to using the site, but ultimately they may still have an impact on the performance of Fan Funding. First, while the lack of a project deadline lowers the barrier to raising funds, it may also limit the funds an individual can raise. A significant amount of data has been collected and analyzed regarding the dynamics of crowdfunding campaigns, and why some succeed while others fail. There appears to be a clear advantage to having a project goal and deadline in place. The combination of a clearly defined project goal and a firm deadline creates a sense of urgency for potential investors and remains a core element of successful crowdfunding campaigns.

Statistically, successful campaigns on sites such as Kickstarter and Indiegogo last between thirty and thirty-five days. More niche focused platforms like TubeStart who accept vetted projects in the filmmaker and videographer verticals only report a fifty day average duration for their most successful campaigns and a higher success rate. It therefore remains to be seen what kind of success rates and funding levels can be achieved without the psychologically important boundaries of a funding goal and campaign deadline.

Ironically, another potential obstacle to YouTube's success may also be its greatest asset: namely its extraordinary level of viewership. While the more than 1 billion viewers boasted by YouTube is difficult to find fault with, it also makes YouTube a very crowded place. And it is a place in which those seeking funds will not only be competing for attention against other funding campaigns, but against the wide, varied, and constantly changing landscape of YouTube content. If this proves to be too much of a distraction, those hoping to engage potential donors in a more substantial manner may decide to choose sites dedicated exclusively to crowdfunding.

Ultimately it comes down to whether or not YouTube's new fundraising feature will change the perception of and expectations from crowdfunding. If it does, it could fundamentally disrupt the entire crowdfunding paradigm.

Implications

YouTube is likely to benefit from its new crowdfunding venture in multiple ways. The most direct benefit may be the new avenue of revenue but ultimately YouTube may also stand to enhance its strongest asset: the volume of its content. Fundraising campaigns have become increasingly elaborate and sophisticated, and often include videos, commercials, and all manner of web content and links, all of which may bolster YouTube's depth of material.

YouTube's move may also promote the use of Google Wallet and Google+. While PayPal holds an anchored marketplace and by almost any reckoning is the standard-bearer of online payments, Google Wallet stands to gain significantly from this move. If Fan Funding gains traction, users are more likely to enjoy the benefits of keeping their campaigning, networking, and funding within the Google universe. And if the "tip jar" approach catches on elsewhere online, this will only add to the use and acceptance of Google Wallet and even Google+, which has long struggled to capture networking market share from Facebook. In fact, given that PayPal also faces a threat from Apple Pay, its future dominance could eventually be endangered by YouTube's crowdfunding launch.

In addition to the potential benefits for YouTube and Google, the individuals using the Fan Funding feature stand to reap great rewards. To some, utilizing a tip jar on a YouTube channel may appear a menial method for raising funds. However, this relatively simple feature may promise significant benefits to launching businesses or accelerating individual users' careers. Recalling the opening vignette, the indie band may capitalize on momentum generated while on tour to create buzz for their band and get noticed by the media, music producers, or other artists. While this is only a single hypothetical example, the manner in which Fan Funding can be used to promote individual's goals is limited only by the creativity of the users themselves; and if the content of YouTube is any indication, that creativity is boundless.

So, what effect might all of this have on the crowdfunding marketplace? Depending upon one's definition of crowdfunding, upwards of 450 such platforms currently exist. While heavyweights such as Kickstarter, Indiegogo, GoFundMe and RocketHub may account for the bulk of the traffic, there is no shortage of niche sites available, and they continue to multiply. YouTube's entrance into the market is likely to stymie the growth of new entrants (at least in the short term) as individuals gain recognition of YouTube's offers and begin to utilize their platform for fundraising. Depending upon whether, and to what extent, the value of YouTube's platform is received, some of the smaller crowdfunding platforms may lose users and ultimately fail.

Changing the crowdfunding paradigm

Even more intriguing than its competitive implications, YouTube's move has the potential to change the very nature of crowdfunding. So far crowdfunding campaigns have been largely defined as time bound and target driven, and the sites that offer crowdfunding have largely been built around supporting that perception. YouTube's model could change that paradigm to one that is adaptive, centralized, and not bound by time.

The key dynamic that YouTube is challenging is the fundamental differentiation between fan building and interaction on one hand, and fundraising and campaigning on the other. It is now widely accepted that the success of crowdfunding depends heavily upon the effective leveraging of one's network base (consisting of one's connections on Facebook, LinkedIn, Google+, Twitter, etc.), and channeling that network over to a fundraising platform. In essence, the crowdfunding model has accepted the premise that network building (or crowd building) is a fundamentally separate process from the crowdfunding process itself. YouTube may begin to challenge that premise.

Having evolved significantly from its early stages as a mere video repository, YouTube now functions as an unparalleled fan-building portal, one in which viewers are independently drawn to the site with the hopes of being entertained, and finding content that they can follow and become a fan of. On the surface, YouTube's Fan Funding feature is by no means profound; it simply gives users a convenient way to accept payments without requiring fans to leave the site. Yet on a deeper level, YouTube may have challenged the premise that a fully dedicated, and separate, crowdfunding platform is necessary. After all, now that consumers have accepted the addition of cameras on their mobile phones, the need for a stand-alone camera has all but disappeared.

Is YouTube merging crowdfunding and crowdsourcing?

Perhaps the most profound impact of YouTube's entry into crowdfunding may be its potential to merge the crowdfunding and crowdsourcing movements. YouTube possesses the capacity to be many things to many users. For some it is merely an entertainment portal for watching funny videos or listening to music. For others it is a site on which they can follow someone's artistic, comedic, or educational work. Regardless of one's intent, and regardless of whether one is a contributor or viewer, the core function of YouTube is to share the contributions of individuals or groups with their chosen community, or even the entire world.

This dynamic capacity suggests that YouTube may have, intentionally or not, ventured into the crowdsourcing space as well. One of the underlying premises of crowdsourcing is that when approaching a problem, there is value in reaching beyond small groups and instead tapping into the experience, expertise, and variety of large crowds. YouTube may have taken its first step in the direction of crowdsourcing as far back as 2008, when, in an attempt to allow users to connect in a more meaningful way with their fans, it launched its Moderator feature. This enables fans to submit questions and suggestions to YouTube channels and then vote them up or down in order to bring their questions to the forefront. This relatively simple capability, coupled with YouTube's massive and engaged audience, provides it with the capacity to become a *crowdfunding* platform that utilizes *crowdsourcing* in the process.

Let's go back to the example of our indie band. If it wants to raise funds to go on tour, it can extend an open call for funds on its YouTube channel, and ask for donations from its fans. And even though YouTube doesn't specifically offer rewards in return, the indie band can creatively include awards as part of its open call. For instance, they could ask their fans which cities they should visit on their tour; fans would then submit their city of choice and collectively vote on their choices. The band could then say that it will visit as many cities as it can given their funding; perhaps it needs $1,000 to reach each destination, so for each thousand-dollar benchmark, the band adds a new city. In essence, the band has crowdfunded on YouTube, and crowdsourced the rewards by creating an open call for suggestions and then linking the level of funding to their ability to reach each city.

Yet from the users' perspective, the key advantage of this merger of crowdfunding and crowdsourcing is not just the crowdsourced rewards, but the continuous nature of the funding. Suppose for instance that the band goes out on tour for its first five shows and delivers a completely awe-inspiring performance that is captured on video, posted to YouTube, and generates a buzz throughout social media. This surge of collective energy among the fan base can be captured and then translated into further donations, and perhaps even additional shows.

The above example is merely a hypothetical example of how YouTube's Fan Funding capacity may transform the current conception of crowdfunding. Could it also lead to a transformation of charitable giving and social movements?

Influence on social movements and charitable giving

YouTube, along with other social media sites such as Facebook and Twitter, has begun playing a significant role in social movements across the globe. In 2012, the events culminating in the "Arab Spring" in Egypt were broadcast throughout the world not just by traditional journalists, but by individuals at the heart of the demonstrations. They communicated in real time by posting text, pictures, and video via every available means of communication. The compelling nature of the unedited videos in particular proved moving to viewers, who were galvanized to take action either by supporting protests in their home countries or by petitioning their government representatives to take action. The power of video sharing platforms such as YouTube was on full display during the Arab Spring, and by most accounts its impact has never been stronger.

With the simple addition of Fan Funding, YouTube has taken the emotive power of real-time video posting and added the capacity for one-click donations to individuals in great need. If video emerges of families in mass exodus attempting to leave areas of conflict, the plight of those affected would likely elicit a response from viewers. In the throes of this emotional reaction, viewers could immediately donate money, which would be transmitted immediately to the individuals in distress.

This enhanced capacity to support social movements may have the tangential effect of making YouTube more controversial in certain parts of the world. The site has already been blocked temporarily or banned permanently in certain regions. For instance, it was dubbed "immoral" and placed under ban in Iran, and it was among several social media sites shut down in countries such as Libya during the Arab Spring. If YouTube becomes a platform for providing financial support to those undertaking social change, then access to the site may become more coveted, and controversial.

The same type of immediate, visceral interaction could transform the nature of charitable giving. In the wake of natural disasters, charitable organizations often emerge to take on the role of raising funds to funnel into local relief efforts. Yet despite the best efforts of some of the most well-intentioned charitable institutions, there is typically not only a time delay between getting funds to individuals in need, but also regrettable fund misallocation. Such impediments may potentially be avoided through the use of donations given through YouTube. In the same way that individuals may solicit funds during periods of political strife, they may also receive support during times of natural disaster.

Thus, the potential implications of YouTube's simple Fan Funding feature appear significant and far reaching. However, the nascent nature of this feature's roll-out and adoption prevent the market from drawing any firm conclusions.

Conclusion

It remains to be seen whether or not YouTube's Fan Funding feature will take hold or recede into the crowded mix of the site's background features. Two key determinants may affect its adoption. First, if advertising revenues suffer due to the challenging click-per-view situation and increased competition from ad-free services, then users may be more apt to adopt Fan Funding and integrate it into their channels. Second, it is still an open question as to whether YouTube content providers feel comfortable asking for donations.

Some early adopters have voiced hesitation about the manner in which it may change their viewers' perceptions of them. However, some popular channels, such as SoulPancake, have welcomed the feature with open arms as another way to fund their creative content.

Beyond the issue of adoption lies the question of the impact that crowdfunding will have on companies such as YouTube, and for that matter, other popular content providers such as Netflix. These industry leaders have succeeded in large part due to their possession of exceptional levels of content provided "on-demand" to viewers. Netflix has recently made the shift from content provider to content creator with its introduction of widely acclaimed series such as *House of Cards* and *Orange is the New Black*. Could crowdfunding on YouTube likewise inspire high-end content creation that is both crowdfunded and crowdsourced?

Perhaps it is too early to answer such questions. But, even if we cannot yet assess the true impact of YouTube's tip jar, the sheer scope and power of the site suggests the potential for it to affect online funding as well as content delivery and creation. The technology community, along with crowdfunding loyalists and the world community at large, will be watching YouTube's crowdfunding foray with great interest.

KIMBERLY-CLARK

Stephen Paljieg, Kimberly-Clark

How do I innovate my way into new areas of business while delivering reliable performance on the core? How can I afford to explore new pathways for growth? How can I afford not to? These challenges are familiar to many of us. Yet new tools and approaches to overcome the challenge of innovating in the increasingly fast paced, ever changing world of today have been shockingly rare.

But there is hope. Through new types of innovation programs, big companies are discovering that it pays to get small.

A new perspective

What role do the consumers of your brand play in helping to create its success? Do they just consume the goods or services you provide or do they add value in other ways?

Challenging and expanding the role for consumers within our brands is not a task we typically take on as marketers. More often than not, our thoughts are focused on optimizing the commercial programs that are designed to act *on* our target audience. We design advertising and promotions that aim to influence the way our consumers think and change the way they act. In the course of pursuing the best way to talk to our consumers, modify their actions, and service their needs, we spend countless hours and dollars on traditional market research studies. These studies often rely on tools and techniques designed with the sole purpose of equipping the brand-building "innovator" with the information that will, we hope, delight the product- or service-consuming "innovatee." In the end, however, it's all about what we do *for* the consumer.

As a result, our innovation labs are largely closed systems. They are somewhat permeable to the needs of the external environment, but only on our terms and only in response to the questions we ask. Within the system boundaries we erect, the resources are limited and so are the number of ideas we see and pursue. We can be so busy innovating in our traditional way that we periodically forget to pause and consider why and how we do the things we do. We ignore a key innovation imperative: to relentlessly innovate the way we innovate.

The happy accident

I can still recall quite clearly the "happy accident" that made us re-examine our approach to innovation on Huggies®, forcing us to acknowledge that "mother knows best," not just in childcare, but also in innovating for child rearing. It set us on a journey that began with crowdsourcing and looks likely to move on towards crowdfunding.

My colleagues and I were in Chicago, Illinois, being put through the paces of a brainstorming exercise to identify and define what we hoped would be some new, profitable places for Huggies® to play in the baby and childcare universe. As part of this process, the innovation consultants we hired had invited several external thought leaders on baby and childcare to the event. We hoped that these thought leaders were smarter about asking moms questions than we were. While they gave us a wealth of interesting information and perspective, none of what we learned unlocked the pathway to the kinds of new opportunities we were looking for at the time.

Then came lunch. During the break, one of the external thought leaders, Maria Bailey, President of BSM Media, approached me. What she said made me ignore the cell phone ringing in my pocket. "You're asking the wrong question," she began. "Instead of trying to figure out how to ask moms what they need, you should be looking at what they are inventing." She was challenging the very fabric of what we were there to do that day. This new way of looking at things both embarrassed and energized me. Could a crowd of entrepreneurial moms really help point the way to new domains for the Huggies® brand? Could the consumers we innovated for become our new partners in innovation? By the time my cell phone stopped ringing, the seed of crowdsourced innovation for Huggies® had been planted.

What Maria told me next sold me on the approach. At the time of our conversation there were over 6 million entrepreneurial moms in the U.S. Seventy-nine percent of these "mompreneurs" developed their ideas after their baby arrived, giving them powerful, first-hand experience and understanding of unmet needs in the baby and childcare category. And yet, like too many women-owned businesses, their enterprises were starved for capital. Less than 3 percent of all financial investments went to the 10 million plus women-owned businesses in the U.S.

We didn't come into to this brainstorming event expecting to create a crowd of mom innovators, but we didn't dismiss the thought as off-topic when it came up. So, how could we enable crowdsourced innovation by mothers, help more moms in business solve more child-rearing problems for other moms, and establish our brand as a curator of innovation rather than simply a leading provider of diapers and wipes? The answer to the question became the Huggies® MomInspired™ program.

The Huggies® MomInspired™ Program

Each year, Huggies® makes an investment in the entrepreneurial community of moms, advancing the cause of these start-up businesses, curating the innovations they produce, and solving problems for moms and babies via the enterprises it supports. Selected mompreneurs get a $15,000 grant, innovation mentoring, a support community in other grant recipients, and perhaps most importantly, validation by one of the premier brands in the baby and childcare universe. Now entering its fifth year, the program boasts a crowd of forty-two grant recipients. Each entrepreneur in this community has an insight, an execution, and a story that confirms our belief that mothers have a unique and compelling take on innovation in this field.

For example, Amy Baxter is a mom, pediatrician, and mompreneur from Atlanta, Georgia. Amy wondered why the administration of a shot had to hurt a child and trouble a mother. Why hadn't anyone else been motivated to solve this problem? It took a mother. Amy's device, Buzzy®, uses the application of vibration and cold to block the nerve impulses associated with the pain of a shot. Numerous clinical studies and medical publications confirm that it works, and Amy is off building her business with a mission to spare children and adults from injection pain.

Lauren Levy struggled to get her infant nephew into his undergarments without pinching his skin in the metal snaps that often just didn't work. Sound familiar? Enter Magnificent Baby®, Lauren's solution to this problem. Lauren substituted small magnets for the mechanical fasteners. It's a simple and effective solution with no pinches and 100 percent reliable fastening. As Lauren's original innovation is rapidly growing in sales and distribution, she has extended this magnetic closure system beyond baby undergarments to clothing, costumes, and other wearable items.

It's common for parents to be told to keep a newborn's umbilical cord uncovered, clean, and dry until it eventually falls off. Yet newborn undergarments, commonly called "onesies," cover up the cord and can make it challenging to clean (especially with a wriggling newborn). Enter Jonelle Krier, a mother and labor delivery room nurse with over twenty years of experience. Her product, Assessables®, is the first undergarment that follows all umbilical cord care standards. It is designed with a simple notch in the garment to allow easy exposure of the umbilical cord. In addition, by making the cord accessible, care can be given without removing the entire garment and making the baby cold and possibly fussy.

Each year since the program's inception, mompreneurs have been invited to apply for a Huggies® MomInspired™ grant at the program's web portal, www.huggiesmominspired. com. Between 400 and 1,000 entrepreneurial moms apply annually and about ten to fifteen of the applicants receive a $15,000 program grant.

The program is not a charity. It is not corporate philanthropy. At its core, it is a commercial relationship between an entrepreneurial mom and the Huggies® brand. It is a relationship intended to build value for both the innovator and the brand. It all starts with a good grant application. Generating good applications is a cornerstone of the program's success. At Huggies® we debated what success would look like. While the number of applications would matter, their quality would matter much more. We wanted to go beyond considering raw ideas, choosing instead to pursue early life-cycle innovations, goods, or services with some level of commercial definition. We seek out proposals that have some line-of-sight to a business plan or even some early, limited sales experience.

Another paramount consideration is protecting the intellectual property of applicants and we employ several approaches to do so. First, we instruct mompreneurs (and more recently "dadpreneurs" too) not to submit any applications for innovations associated with diapers or wipes, the core Huggies® business. Doing so allows us to avoid any overlap, real or perceived, between our internal innovation program and the Huggies® MomInspired™ program. It also helped to convince the internal innovation community at Kimberly-Clark that we were not out to replace them or their efforts, but rather to complement their work with external innovations that could help us expand our brand footprint.

Second, we have applicants complete an online confidential disclosure agreement (CDA) prior to entering the application portal. This agreement protects both them and us, and sets the expectations for the consideration and grant process. We thought our Kimberly-Clark legal team was crazy when they first proposed it. Just how many mompreneurs would we turn away when they saw that the first step on our web portal was the review and digital signature of a legal document? Well, we've been proven wrong. All the feedback we've gathered from grant applicants has told us that the online CDA gave them the basic assurance that we were not going to steal their innovations. It also demonstrates that we recognize them and treat them like the businesswomen they are or aspire to be. Kudos to our lawyers for creating a user-friendly and respectful document, in line with the tone of our program.

At the end of the application period, a small team, usually three to five people, reviews all the submissions. Limiting access at this stage helps us to act with discretion to protect the interests of grant applicants and, of course, Huggies®. Applications are carefully reviewed not just for their obvious innovation potential but also for the quality of their business model thinking and their fit with the promise of our brand to "liberate the joy of parenting." The act of reading these applications actually provides Huggies® with the first tangible reward of the program, as they offer a lesson from the marketplace about moms' points of pain and the solutions being pursued. It is free market and "free" market research untentacled by traditional methods or approaches. If we're good observers, this crowd of applicants can teach us a lot about the markets we serve through the innovations they are pursuing.

A select number of applicants, the best of the best, are chosen to be Huggies® MomInspired™ grant recipients. Making the notification calls to new recipients is just about the best professional experience ever. In all cases, callers understand that they are making a fundamental difference to their prospects. Many times we have been told by grant recipients that they were about to give up on their dreams before our program came along. Sure, the tangible benefits of the program mattered, but what counted even more was that a brand that they knew and loved recognized their work and told them that it had value.

What does a grant recipient receive? First, she is extended a $15,000 grant. No specific instructions are provided on how the grant should be used, we only ask that it be utilized to advance the business prospects of her enterprise. We recognized that a "big company" telling a small entrepreneur how to behave was most probably a recipe for failure. Brands like Huggies® are very good at being big and pretty poor at acting small.

Second, a grant recipient gets access to our brand equity

with the award of a specific program trademark badge. This badge can be used on-pack, on her website, and in her sales materials to show the celebration of her product or service by Huggies®. Grant recipients have consistently cited this element as the most valuable of all program benefits, as it has shown to be a door-opener, conversation-starter, and deal-closer for many a key commercial conversation. Recently, we have also taken to representing the program at the All Baby & Child Kids Expo, the biggest trade show in the baby and childcare industry, providing an invaluable opportunity for grant recipients to connect with retailers and other well-known brands.

Third, a program mompreneur gets access to relevant knowledge. Small business operational and strategic information is provided free of charge on our website. Several mentoring relationships have been set up between Huggies® employees and grant recipients. One of the most successful arrangements was in the area of package design where a program mom was facing the challenge of redesigning her primary packaging. We linked her up with a Kimberly-Clark design manager who was able to coach and mentor her on some key design principles. She was delighted and learned a lot. We also gained an unanticipated pick-up as the design manager caught the entrepreneur spark and gained a renewed passion for innovation.

Last, all grant recipients benefit from the community we help construct and the connections they initiate between themselves. Beyond emotional support, not to be easily dismissed given the rocky road of the entrepreneur, members of our community support each other in the basic tasks associated with successfully advancing an innovation. If a program mom needs to file a patent and hasn't done so before, another grant recipient is there to show her how. If a mompreneur is looking to develop a sourcing plan, someone else will share her work and relevant experiences.

But how does the brand win? Let's not forget that the key to a sustainable crowdsourced innovation program is commercial success for all involved. Huggies® wins in two ways. The first is by gaining access to new innovations that can advance the expansion of the brand into new domains. We see high quality ideas developed by real moms with first-hand experiences in child rearing. Innovations of this kind often go undiscovered by companies vested in traditional development programs and the market research tools they employ. By journeying forward with these moms and checking in periodically on the success of their businesses, our company gives these smart bets a chance to mature into enterprises which can create new commercial value for all.

Meet Allyson Phillips, a mompreneur from San Diego, California and one of our original grant recipients. Allyson is the inventor of the Tilty Cup™, an inspired reinvention of the sippy cup and the first true training cup for toddlers. We've all had experience with sippy cups, either directly or by watching the toddler drinking experience through the eyes of a frustrated mom. How do sippy cups fall short of the task they are designed for? They all require the toddler to turn the cup upside-down, 180 degrees overhead, to get the last bit of liquid out. And what toddler doesn't want that last bit of apple juice? Inevitably the liquid inside spills, the lid of the cup falls off, or both happen.

Allyson had a better way. By smartly manipulating the internal geometry of a sippy cup, she constrained the liquid flow in such a way that the last bit of liquid came out when the cup was at a much more reasonable angle, say the angle that a normal adult drinks from a glass or cup. Eureka! No spills. No messes. Happy toddlers. Happier mothers. For the first time ever moms can buy a sippy cup that tutors toddlers in the drinking ergonomics we practice as adults. The first true "teaching cup" was born. So too says the U.S. Patent Office, which granted Allyson a utility patent on her innovation.

Can you tell I like the Tilty Cup™? But more importantly, so does Evenflo Feeding, a Kimberly-Clark subsidiary, and a business in search of new ideas to reset its toddler feeding accessories business. It is an innovation marriage made in heaven, so much so that Evenflo Feeding has completed a licensing agreement with Allyson for the rights to manufacture and sell Tilty Cup™ throughout the Americas. Allyson has gone big time and Evenflo Feeding has gotten the innovation they so desperately sought.

What's the return on investment of this innovation tale? For a $15,000 grant investment, Kimberly-Clark, through its Evenflo Feeding Subsidiary, gains access to an innovation which will grow the top line of its toddler feeding business by several million dollars (less Allyson's royalties, of course).

How does Huggies® protect its ability to make a commercial deal with these small businesses at some later point in time? It does so by asking for one, and only one, consideration from recipients in return for all the program benefits. That consideration is a simple right of first refusal. The obligation is not to do a deal exclusively with Huggies®, but simply the commitment to talk to the brand first; this ensures that we have a preferred position in any future deal flows.

The second way that the program builds value for Huggies® is by the advocacy of its participants and the recognition of moms in general who see the good the brand is doing. Since its inception, over 100 million brand impressions (times when consumers talk about our brand) have been attributed to our program. Each and every one of those impressions has something good to say about the brand and the work that Huggies® is doing with its crowd of inventive moms. And those impressions are very cost-effective with the cost per thousand impressions running 40 percent below what traditional marketing programs can deliver.

From crowdsourcing to crowdfunding

It is frequently said that "necessity is the mother of invention." At Huggies® we've learned that "moms are necessary inventors." Fueled by their dual commitments to motherhood and invention, mompreneurs are developing the new products and services that address the pressing child rearing needs of today with an insight and acumen that large companies often lack. We've been smart enough to see the value in this mompreneurial crowd and have used the Huggies® MomInspired™ program to crowdsource innovation for our brand and create a better future for our inspired partners.

We are innovating in a new age. Never before have those we serve as marketers had the capability to innovate for themselves. Consumers now have the capacity to develop meaningful new products and services and make them widely available to others in need.

We can already see a future where company and consumer collaborate to crowdsource innovations that help define the brands they both love. Now let's go one step further. Imagine the role that crowdfunding could play. By inviting the crowd to invest and vote with their dollars on the merits of a proposition, entrepreneurs and their corporate investors would get an even earlier read on the merits of an innovation. Financial risk would be diversified and investors from the crowd would become an early adopter population for the new good or service. New bonds would be forged between companies and consumers as together they define the future for categories—if not entire markets.

How will we as brand builders respond to this explosion of innovation potential? Will it be the source of new innovation that inspires us? Or will it lead to our lack of relevancy and eventual demise? I choose to be an optimist. By recognizing the innovation occurring outside our walls, by embracing the crowd and its many talents, we can create an innovation environment where both the entrepreneur and brand win.

THE SPORTS INDUSTRY

Erit Yellen, Orna Drive Productions

Former National Football League running back T.J. Duckett hails from Kalamazoo, Michigan. He attended college at Michigan State University in East Lansing, was drafted in the first round to the Atlanta Falcons in 2004, then went on to play for the Washington Redskins, Detroit Lions, and Seattle Seahawks, until he retired and settled back in East Lansing, Michigan in 2009.

In each city that he played, T.J. was able to create fans, relationships, and a loyal following for his charitable efforts, performed wherever he was playing at the time as well as back in Michigan, and even in Kenya. However, there was no platform that he could use to bring all of these people together. Local events can often be cumbersome and prohibitively costly and they can also exclude the hundreds of fans and supporters from all over the globe that have come to know and support T.J. and his causes.

T.J. is just one of many athletes (and brands) in sports to encounter this problem, and he like others has discovered that crowdfunding is part of the solution. In this "insider view" we will discuss specific crowdfunding campaigns run by individual professional athletes, professional sports teams, athlete foundations, global non-profit organizations, and large sports-based corporations. Each campaign is unique in its outreach, call to action and messaging. Each has had its own success, not just in money raised but also in information acquired for future fundraising, marketing, and public relations strategies. Together they represent just the beginning of crowdfunding in sports, and the impact that it will have on the industry.

Right To Play

Right To Play is a global humanitarian organization that uses sport to help teach children important lessons about health, education, and conflict resolution. It was founded in 2002 by former Norwegian speed skater Johann Olav Koss, who won gold medals at the Winter Olympics in 1992 and 1994, and by the end of 2013 its programs had reached over a million children in over twenty countries.

The Right To Play organization uses professional athletes to help it raise funds and awareness; in fact its U.S. operation has close to ninety such ambassadors on its roster. However, due to their individual training regimes, competition schedules, and personal commitments, these ambassadors tend to be spread out all over the globe, making it difficult for them to help as much or as often as they would like. It was to solve this problem that Right To Play turned to the crowdfunding platform Indiegogo.

For five months, Right To Play worked hard to get the campaign ready to launch. They decided to build it around the fact that 2014 represented the twentieth anniversary of its founder's gold medal success at the Winter Olympics in Lillehammer. They called the campaign "20 for 20 for 20," the idea being to use twenty athlete ambassadors to raise enough money to help 20,000 more children before the end of the twentieth anniversary year. They filmed twenty professional athletes, such as gymnast Gabby Douglas, swimmer Nathan Adrian, sprinter Allyson Felix, and soccer player Heather O'Reilly, all of whom were asked to recite the same script. A three-minute video was then edited together featuring all of the athletes and this formed the basis for the campaign's launch on Indiegogo. The date chosen was December 2, 2013, timed to coincide with "Giving Tuesday" (an annual day of online charitable giving designed to fall just after Thanksgiving).

Each athlete ambassador was asked to donate to the campaign personally, but also to reach out to friends, family, and fans with pre-drafted emails and then to post social media messages and images throughout the course of the campaign. It proved to be a winning formula. The campaign garnered widespread national attention in the U.S., featuring on Mashable.com and on *USA Today*'s "For the Win" website. Fans and donors were asked to donate specific amounts ranging from $10 or $25 all the way up to $5,000 in exchange for both athlete-based perks (like tickets to a San Francisco 49ers game) or program-based perks ($50 would buy one child the gift of play for an entire year in Right To Play programs).

In the end the campaign had over 10,000 views from over thirty countries around the world. Its initial goal was to raise $100,000 on the site itself, of which they raised approximately $78,000. But because donors and athletes were so inspired by the campaign, the organization received an additional $40,000 into the office bringing the total to about $120,000.

Not only did the campaign give Right To Play the opportunity to raise money; it also gave this large group of athletes and supporters a way that they could help like never before. The campaign helped raise awareness for an organization that struggles to gain coverage in the United States; it led to the creation of unique content which could be shared across multiple other platforms; and it delivered valuable information on existing and potential donors and supporters.

It was such a success that Indiegogo uses it as an example of how to construct, launch, and run a campaign in the cause and non-profit space. It should also prove invaluable when Right To Play reaches out to its corporate sponsors with further ideas for the use of crowdfunding.

Project Brabham

In 1948 motor racing legend Sir Jack Brabham started up a Formula 1 racing team in Sydney, Australia. In 1966, Brabham went on to become the first and only driver in history to win a Formula 1 World Championship in a car of his own. He was world-renowned for being one of the best racers and engineers on the circuit and his team became a firm fans' favourite. It continued to dominate the sport into the 1980s until it had to fold due to lack of funding.

Some twenty years later, Brabham's son David is attempting to bring a new Brabham Racing Team back to the track. He decided to use the crowdfunding platform Indiegogo to raise funds, test the market, and let fans know about his plans. The initial goal of the campaign was to raise £250,000 ($390,000), which would help fund the first round of developing an outreach program that would allow the team to engineer new cars and train new drivers.

In return for donations, Project Brabham promised "access to the inner workings of a race team from its early days of development, revealing information that is normally a closely guarded secret" and "the ability to vote on certain team decisions from the outset." It also set up a knowledge-sharing and e-learning portal called "Brabham-Digital" to allow interested fans, drivers, and engineers (amateur and professional) to progress their own skills in the sport. Funders could purchase membership to the portal under three different categories: Brabham Fan, Brabham Engineer, and Brabham Driver. All provided tailored access to the process of creating the new team. The campaign was also transparent in communicating that the more momentum they received through the crowdfunding campaign, the more corporate backing they would get.

In the end, Project Brabham exceeded its funding goal by raising £278,000 ($437,500) from over 3,000 donors— the most successful example of for-profit crowdfunding in the sports industry to date. It also received extensive media coverage in the UK and in racing publications. It is an exciting example of how a long-defunct brand can completely reinvent itself by using crowdfunding to tap into a nostalgic, engaged, and enthusiastic fan base.

Jamaican Women's Soccer Team

In 2008 the Jamaican Women's Soccer Team, affectionately referred to as "The Reggae Girlz" was disbanded due to lack of funding. In the spring of 2014, the Jamaican Football Federation (JFF) decided to bring the team back together to make a run at the 2015 Women's World Cup. Jamaican soccer players who were competing overseas in Europe, the United States, and Canada all came home in the hope of making it through six months of training and qualifying tournaments. Usually other national teams get years to train and compete together, but the Reggae Girlz were hopeful and driven to do the best they could.

When word first got out that the Reggae Girlz were re-forming and that they needed help with raising funds, the JFF fielded an approach from Cedella Marley, daughter of reggae star Bob Marley. Cedella runs many of the Marley family's businesses and brands and thought she could help to promote the team via the different Marley platforms. The JFF duly appointed Cedella as the Ambassador of the Reggae Girlz in late spring of 2014.

Luckily for the Reggae Girlz, their new ambassador was incredibly business savvy. Her experience running record labels and overseeing the trademark and licensing of the Marley family name had introduced her to the power of crowdfunding, which she knew had worked well in the music business over the last few years. She therefore decided to create an initial campaign to help the Reggae Girlz with training costs and travel costs for their first qualifying tournament. It was a deliberately small-scale start; Cedella knew that multiple crowdfunding campaigns were going to be part of the answer to build fundraising levels and global awareness for the Reggae Girlz. The campaigns would also give the girls on the team a tool to help the cause by engaging their outer circles of family, friends, and fans.

The original campaign proved relatively simple to set up via the GoFundMe platform, but the team became frustrated that it didn't allow them to showcase their campaign video and offered only limited options for support from potential donors. They therefore chose to run a second campaign via the Indiegogo platform. This incorporated multiple perk levels that were able to reap the benefits of the Marley family's direct businesses such as Tuff Gong Records and Marley Coffee as well as cherished partners like Bravado clothing, Island Records, and House of Marley. It was also an opportunity to highlight the strength of the Marley social media platforms that included fourteen different sites with an astounding 80 million followers, not including the platforms offered by all of the other partner companies.

The hope was that by accessing the Marley fan base, the campaign would create enough awareness to pick up donors from across the globe as well as at home in Jamaica. Whether there would be much crossover between this broader fan base and supporters of the soccer team remained to be seen.

Central to the campaign was a three-minute video, carefully crafted to showcase the culture of Jamaica along with powerful testimonials from the Reggae Girlz. Cedella was also featured both on camera as well as in voice-over, and of course a few Bob Marley songs were used. Its high quality meant that it could be used as a stand-alone tool in promotion, marketing, and public relations. The story made it into local Jamaican media, and further afield into *Rolling Stone* and *People* magazines, Mashable.com, Fox Sports, and NBC Sports.

Between the GoFundMe and Indiegogo platforms, the Reggae Girlz raised close to $200,000 for the team through a combination of individual donors and major corporate support. Unfortunately the Reggae Girlz did not make it through qualification to reach the 2015 World Cup, but the success of the crowdfunding campaign has encouraged the team to push for full funding going forward. They were particularly pleased at the level of corporate sponsorship that they attracted, all of whom were happy to be associated with the good will that the campaign generated. Many of the Marley partner companies, for example, donated items themselves to use as perks as well as covering additional shipping costs. The Marley family too has pledged to continue to advocate for the Reggae Girlz in the hope of securing funding for the team to train throughout the year without the fear of having to disband. In that respect, the crowdfunding campaigns have helped to get the soccer team's story heard and provided an international fan base on which future campaigns can build.

Dick's Sporting Goods

The budgets for sports programs in the U.S. have been drastically cut over the last few decades to the point where 60 percent of school children now need to pay if they want to play—most of them in low-income communities. To help combat this problem, the country's largest sporting goods chain, Dick's Sporting Goods, set up a foundation to support programs that inspire and enable sports participation.

In 2014 the Dick's Sporting Goods Foundation worked with Crowdtilt (now Tilt) to establish a bespoke crowdfunding platform in support of a new campaign called "Sports Matter." Its aim was to raise funds and awareness for these youth sports programs and to match community donations with up to $2 million of the company's own money. The platform was also designed to collect and analyze donor and consumer information, which Dick's could then use for future fundraising campaigns.

From February to March 2014, the Sports Matter site encouraged applications from youth programs and teams that wanted to take part in the campaign. Applications were accepted from a total of 184 teams, some unable to continue playing because of funding challenges, some facing closure, and others seeking sufficient funds to begin operating at all. The successful applicants were given training in how to use Dick's crowdfunding platform to tell their own stories and on how to make best use of social media to attract donations (knowledge that might help them with future fundraising efforts too).

Then in mid-April the Sports Matter campaign was launched, with the sports goods chain bringing its full marketing and public relations weight to bear in support of each of the 184 individual teams taking part. First up, the launch itself was held at SxSW's first SXsports Summit. This provided an ideal platform to place the issue of the decline of youth sports in front of key influencers, many of whom chose to publicize the campaign via their own social channels.

Dick's then used hundreds of geo-targeted social media posts to alert communities about local teams taking part in the campaign. All of its PR and marketing efforts drove potential donors to the teams' pages on the crowdfunding platform, where a simple turnkey mechanism allowed them to make donations. The use of a crowdfunding approach also made it easier for Dick's employees, executives, and customers to contribute to the campaign. Celebrity athletes, in particular, were encouraged to tell their fans about particular teams hoping to raise funds from the campaign.

The results were astounding. Over the course of five weeks, the campaign garnered 377 million combined social and PR impressions. More than 340 celebrity influencers helped to drive over 280,000 website visits and 600,000 unique online and point of sale donations. A total of $2 million was raised, with Dick's pledging the same amount again to take the final figure to $4 million.

"We were pleased with the results," says Ryan Eckel, VP of Brand Marketing at Dick's Sporting Goods. "A hundred percent of the teams were fully funded... and have the resources they need to play sports for their next season. We will take key learnings from this first Sports Matter program and improve future campaigns."

The Sports Matter campaign stands out for the amount it raised, the good will it generated, the engagement it enabled between the company and hundreds of thousands of supporters, and the spotlight it shone on the broader issue of sports participation and funding. Dick's decision to create a bespoke crowdfunding platform was a particularly innovative step—recognition that the foundation could inject more money into sports by acting as a platform than it could by simply being a donor.

Jamaican Men's Bobsled Team

Remember the 1993 Disney film *Cool Runnings*? It was a big hit based on the true story of how the Jamaican men's bobsled team tried to qualify and compete in the 1988 Calgary Winter Olympics. Back then, the team's only way of raising money to help them train was through selling t-shirts, and one of the athletes ended up selling his own car to keep the team on track.

Fast forward to the 2014 Winter Olympics in Sochi. The next generation of Jamaica bobsledders had qualified for competition, but had no funding to get themselves or their equipment to the games. In search of a solution, they turned to a few crowdfunding sites to see if they could raise the $100,000 they needed to pay for their travel, equipment, lodging, and food.

Almost overnight the team raised close to $190,000 across two crowdfunding campaigns. Over 4,500 individuals pledged donations and only 20 percent of them were of Jamaican origin, showcasing the widespread affection generated by the *Cool Runnings* film. The team made it to the games and now hopes to use its crowdfunding momentum to continue to train and compete annually in global competition. And to complete the circle, one of the original 1988 bobsledders, Devon Harris, is now helping the current team to become a fully sustainable entity.

Fencing in the Schools

Tim Morehouse, a U.S. silver medalist in fencing, is one of the sport's most influential advocates. He works tirelessly to promote it around the world and is a particular believer in its importance for youth. In 2011, he founded Fencing in the Schools (FITS), a non-profit organization to "empower youth to achieve excellence through the sport of fencing." FITS programs bring the sport into schools to improve education, foster the Olympic ideals, and help fight childhood obesity.

In Spring 2014 FITS was planning a large fundraiser called "Duel for the Schools." The event would be held in New York city and would feature live fencing demonstrations and participation by Olympic fencers. However, FITS wanted to tap into more than just its New York-based donors and supporters. It needed a way to reach out to its wider geographic base in states like Idaho, Illinois, New Jersey, Maine, Washington DC, and Connecticut.

To solve the problem FITS decided to use CrowdRise to run a crowdfunding campaign leading up to the Duel for the School event. Tim and his staff of volunteers spent a few months setting up the campaign, trying to ensure that they would have all of their marketing, fundraising, and PR pieces in place to reach a pre-event target of $150,000. As it turned out, the FITS campaign raised over $175,000—by far the largest athlete-managed crowdfunding campaign to date.

It helped that Tim and FITS already had some crowd-funding experience and were able to apply the lessons they had learned from two previous campaigns. It was this experience, for example, that helped Tim understand how a successful campaign needs months of planning and strategic marketing to generate and maintain momentum. It also led to his decision to engage other corporate sponsors like Sabra Hummus, UnderArmour, and the Dick's Sporting Goods Sports Matter campaign (as it qualified to be a benefiting organization). "We would never have 1,000 donors just with our own fundraising campaign," explains Morehouse. "It took a crowdfunding campaign with matching donations from Dicks's Sports Matter campaign and UnderArmour to create the sort of viral effect we were looking for."

During the FITS campaign, UnderArmour did a "$5 for every $1" donated in a 48-hour period. At the same time, Dick's Sports Matter campaign was doing a "1:1" match. So if a donor went onto the site during those forty-eight hours, every $1 raised was like raising $7. FITS made sure to really push that message out on their social media plat-forms, eblasts, and via additional personal phone calls to get donors to give again or donors who had not yet given, to give during those two days. That forty-eight-hour period alone helped to raise more than 50 percent of the campaign's goal.

For FITS the crowdfunding campaign also created an opportunity to cultivate new donors and to reach out to the fencing community abroad as well as domestically and regionally in the United States. It also gave a sense of empowerment to the schools involved in the organization's programs, encouraging them to raise money and to feel further engaged with the sport of fencing as a whole.

Classroom Champions

Founded by Steve Mesler, a U.S. bobsled gold medalist, Classroom Champions is a non-profit foundation based both in Canada and the United States. Its mission is to connect top performing athletes with students in high-need schools. It uses video lessons and live video chat to motivate students to recognize their potential, set goals, and dream big, while educating them in the practical use of communications technology.

To date, Classroom Champions has run three crowdfunding campaigns, learning valuable lessons on how to make effective use of strategy and communications tools to achieve its fundraising targets. Its first campaign was actually the first time that the organization had ever asked its networks for money. The campaign was partly intended to test Classroom Champions' own fundraising skills. Expectations were low and it was uncertain whether anyone would give anything at all, but in the end, the organization raised $7,500 against an original goal of $4,600. It was a good practice run and made the team more comfortable about mounting another campaign.

However, the second campaign proved to be a bit more difficult. The goal was set much higher at $18,000—an arbitrary figure based on little firm strategizing and too much input from "too many cooks in the kitchen." The campaign, which was also run over a period of six weeks instead of four, eventually brought in only $10,000—missing the target, but an increase on the first campaign.

The third campaign shows the value of experience. This time, Classroom Champions made a few key changes. They narrowed their fundraising efforts down to just their U.S. base, set a lower target of $10,000, and ran the campaign over a more manageable four weeks. They also used an online store to deliver perks more quickly to donors, which meant that many donors received their perks while the campaign was still live and could gain more attention for the campaign by tweeting about them. Classroom Champions also made sure to have $10,000 of matched donations in place and learned from the Right To Play campaign about how to make effective use of their ambassador athletes to help promote the crowdfunding efforts (athletes were added to the campaign as team members, and were given sample emails and tweets to send to their donor base). The result was a final total of $22,000, which will help Classroom Champions reach 1,500 students in the short term and many thousands more further down the line.

Classroom Champions will continue to fine-tune their crowdfunding campaigns and use them as a way to raise funds, generate awareness, and continue to build a support base for their organization.

Individual athletes

Even as this "insider view" was being written, several more crowdfunding campaigns and platforms have been set up.

Interestingly, a number of them are designed to raise funds for individual athletes:

RallyMe.com

This site is for athletes looking to raise money to cover their training costs. It is the official crowdfunding platform for the U.S. governing bodies of twelve different sports, including bobsled, skeleton, speedskating, skiing, snowboarding, and cycling. Many athletes from the 2014 Sochi Winter Olympics used this platform to help them raise money to train and travel as the stipends they typically receive from the U.S. Olympic Committee are just not enough to get them to where they need to be. Corporate sponsorship is also rare and usually kept to a small percentage of Olympic athletes, meaning that many of them need to turn to friends, family, and fans for financial help.

Circling the Wagon for Darryl Talley

After an article was published in Buffalo, NY, about the awful depression afflicting former NFL player Darryl Talley, a single fan decided to start a crowdfunding campaign on GoFundMe.com for Darryl and his family. As of the beginning of December 2014 the campaign had raised close to $150,000 from around 3,000 donors in just five days. The campaign received coverage from media platforms like ESPN, Yahoo!, Fox Sports, and *USA Today*, and reached an amazingly loyal and sympathetic fan base for a former athlete in his fifties whose illness has left him struggling to pay his bills and keep a roof over his family's head.

FanPay.org

This is a crowdfunding site designed to help student athletes raise money for expenses that are not otherwise covered by their scholarships. It has proved controversial because, according to the rules of the National Collegiate Athletic Association (NCAA), student athletes cannot receive donations or make over a certain amount of money. As a result of its activities, the site has received over 100 cease and desist letters, and has gained huge national attention.

The site has tried to get around the NCAA rules by saying that the donations are held in trust until the student graduates. They are therefore "rewards" for graduation—disbursed after the individual ceases to be a student. However, the NCAA has continued to object and, as of writing, the site is accepting donation-rewards for all students *except* student-athletes. It's a case that looks set to run and run.

Conclusion

Crowdfunding is thought of primarily as a way of raising money, and the campaigns above show that it does indeed have the power to generate significant financial results in the sporting world. But it's also obvious that the benefits run more deeply. A good crowdfunding campaign reaches out beyond a cause's traditional supporter base; it gives fans the chance to do more than just donate (by acting as promoters of the campaign to their own networks of friends, family, and colleagues); it brings an issue to the attention of the media, and provides content to make such media coverage easier and more effective; and it gathers data on campaign views and donations that can inform future fundraising and other marketing strategies.

The crowdfunding campaigns mentioned above are just a fraction of the thousands that currently exist. Each day more and more amateur and professional athletes, non-profits, and corporations involved in sports are realizing that crowdfunding, when done right, is an extremely strong tool to engage their fan bases. A few years ago, social media proved to be a game changer in the sports industry. Now it looks like crowdfunding is doing the same, enhancing the connections between athletes, teams, corporations, and the crowds of fans following sports of every kind around the world.

3

CROWDFUNDING AND INNOVATION

Richard Swart

Crowdfunding has incredible potential to transform the different aspects of a corporation's activities. In this section we look at how certain companies are adapting crowdfunding mechanisms to spur innovation, both internally and externally, and to transform the process of product launches, especially for consumer products and goods.

When used creatively, crowdfunding can radically alter the way that corporations engage with their customers. Through the process of offering novel product ideas for sale before they are actually manufactured—a "pre-retailing" model—firms are able to learn massive amounts from their customer base. Each of the customers effectively becomes a member of an enormous focus group, engaged with the firm in a collaborative product design process. However, what really sets this process apart from other methods of product research and development is that the feedback received is reinforced by the customer's willingness to spend their hard-earned cash. In other words, they are putting their money where their mouth is. Through crowdfunding, firms have the opportunity to get quality input from customers who are emotionally and financially invested in the product, to share content with them, and ask questions about the products being offered through crowdfunding. This allows firms to mine the social stream for intelligence about product features and benefits that gain traction among specific demographics.

On the one side, crowdfunding allows potential backers to ask questions, make recommendations, and react to the proposed product or service. On the other, it allows firms to engage current or potential customers through multiple channels and hold discussions with them about desired product features, perceived benefits, and even novel applications of the firm's technologies and products. This creates the potential to pivot a product in a new direction and can sometimes even lead to the creation of a new product altogether.

Fostering innovation

It's not hard to see how this use of the crowdfunding process can lead to such innovation. Imagine being able to connect product designers and engineers with potential customers in ongoing conversations and discussions—with the added benefit that the customers perceive they are valued by the firm. Customers choose to engage through their interest in the initiative or product, removing the contrived environment of a focus group and allowing a natural exchange of ideas motivated by curiosity and ingenuity. By bringing customers into the development process in this way firms are creating a stronger, more dedicated, more loyal client-base and enriching their R&D process into the bargain.

Crowdfunding can also address another of the perceived challenges of new product development—the need to gain early feedback from potential customers without providing too much information to potential competitors. The Sony case study later in this chapter demonstrates that corporate incubators and venture partners can use crowdfunding to test markets without revealing the brand identity of the firm. This approach allows firms to test market reactions to a new product anonymously, reducing the risk involved in a potential launch and providing feedback that could help accelerate the product's market entry. It's a particularly useful tool for large corporations, which are uniquely well set up to exploit market opportunities, and manage the pricing, marketing, packaging, and distribution challenges that beset many start-ups.

It is important to understand that backers of projects or purchasers of goods or services through crowdfunding are not necessarily external to the firm. Crowdfunding dynamics can also be used to transform open innovation processes into highly connected and engaged collaborations among co-workers. These processes all accelerate or improve existing mechanisms of innovation. Crowdfunding essentially connects and synergizes different company activities; it provides the mechanisms through which marketing, PR, product development, and other functions can all support and augment each other, thereby improving efficiency and optimization.

It's a process that has benefits for both employees and employer. By using some kind of crowdfunding mechanism, an employer can encourage employees to share their ideas, give them a path to success that also benefits the company, and take advantage of the many ideas people have as a by-product of their work, tapping a source that can otherwise be overlooked. And the mechanism itself allows these ideas to arise from a mutual interaction with coworkers, creating a feeling of camaraderie but also a sense of competition and value. This makes participation and engagement much more likely than by using a traditional suggestion box or an open-door policy.

When using crowdfunding to mine ideas from the public a similar mechanism can be used to offer people the chance to get their idea funded if it is successful. By allowing people to submit their ideas and using company resources to develop successful ones, the company gains IP rights and potential partners from successfully funded ventures, and an influx of other ideas which may lead to new products or the improvement of existing ones somewhere down the line.

When a company is looking to outsource innovation by investing in a start-up or buying a company, crowdfunding can also be an excellent tool for evaluation. In addition to being a good indicator of where a target company is at in terms of its development, crowdfunding provides real market validation and proof-of-concept. And by using crowdfunding as another measuring device, companies can reduce their risk and minimize the chances of a failed investment.

It's also worth noting that crowdfunding is not limited to financing of innovation by corporations. The ABN AMRO case study in this chapter demonstrates how a major bank launched a very successful crowdfunding program to help fund external companies with a social mission. As a result, the bank helped grow the innovation ecosystem, built good will among start-ups, provided opportunities for investors, and helped develop future banking relationships.

Engagement is the key

The common theme across all of these examples and case studies is that innovation is the product of engagement. Great ideas can spring from almost anything—the theory of gravity was reputedly inspired by an apple falling on someone's head—but in reality, inventions are rarely the product of just one idea. It takes many great ideas, each building on the insights of the previous ones, to create something new. Often these ideas come from different sources. As Paul Brody points out in his case study (see page 187), research has shown that the most valuable ideas for innovation come from outside firms. Crowdfunding mechanisms acccelerate this process.

There are those who believe that a collective of people will always be smarter than an individual, no matter how intelligent he or she is. Whether or not that's true, it is certainly evident that a group of people can often come up with solutions and ways of thinking that a single person would not achieve on their own. This is because each individual in the group brings their own experiences, skills, outlook, and values to the mix and each member is further capable of original thought in reaction to other information and input from the group. And the larger the group, the greater this pool of information and ideas becomes.

Innovation is at its most prolific and most efficient when it is a collaborative process, benefiting from deeper connections to the ecosystem and market. Crowdfunding creates social cohesion—connecting innovators and experts outside the company with the company itself—and, when used as an internal mechanism, creating insightful connections between employees too. The bottom line is that the process of social outreach by the company in promoting the campaign allows it to discover innovative thinkers, new technologies, and individual interactions that no amount of market research would otherwise have uncovered. The lesson, therefore, is simple: a smart company knows that its customers are more than just consumers and its workers are more than just employees; they can also be partners for innovation and if treated as such, they can become an important asset—a crowd asset.

SONY

Dan Marom and Kevin Berg Grell

The Kickstarter campaign launched by Pebble Technologies for its e-paper watch (see page 14) challenged the common perception that crowdfunding is a seed-funding alternative, with limited potential for larger companies. It was the first campaign to raise $1 million in one day, and to exceed $10 million in total funding, all within a period of just thirty-seven days.

In 2014, technology giant Sony duly launched a crowdfunding campaign for its own FES e-paper watch. It may prove to be the beginning of a wider innovation strategy for the company, which integrates market validation all the way back to the idea stage—just as we see with the use of crowdfunding by start-ups. Whether or not Sony will go on to apply crowdfunding to its remaining product pipeline is yet to be seen, but its first foray into the field is being watched with interest by its competitors, by companies of a similar size in different industries, and by the crowdfunding industry itself.

A rite of passage

In *Silicon Republic*, award-winning technology journalist, John Kennedy, described Sony's crowdfunding initiative as a small component of a major development within the company. He argues that Sony is in the midst of a strategic

change that will lead to a stricter focus on the profit genera-
tors in the company's portfolio.

For corporate innovation, strategic changes such as this
often spell cut-backs and very limited bandwidth in terms
of exploring new opportunities and markets. For Sony, this
is not the case; the company will simply streamline the
innovation pipeline, and with the crowdfunding campaign
for the FES e-paper watch, it seems they have found a way
to tap market interest as well. This substantially lowers the
cost of market research, and it gives the company an opportunity to get early feedback on their product idea.

The FES e-paper watch campaign was launched on
the crowdfunding platform makuake.com, and reached
its goal fairly quickly. The campaign owner was Fashion
Entertainments—a spin-off Sony division—and according
to the *Wall Street Journal*, the reason that Sony's brand was
not included in the campaign material was that the company wanted clear and unbiased feedback on the product
alone. "We hid Sony's name because we wanted to test the
real value of the product, whether there will be demand for
our concept," according to one of the people involved with
the campaign.

The idea of testing the waters via crowdfunding is not
new. Start-up entrepreneurs (especially in the B2C space)
are expected to have some market validation before seeking angel or venture capital. Crowdfunding has provided
a means to that end. What is new is that a large enterprise like Sony has found a way of benefiting from the same
mechanism.

There were rumors about Sony's e-paper watch throughout 2014, and a general interest in the company's innovation strategy. By reducing the focus on smartphones and TVs as a part of the company's new strategy, Sony's future revenues will rely heavily on PlayStation and cameras. This sends a clear signal to product developers within the company as well as externally. Marketability drives Sony's portfolio.

In this context, the e-paper campaign fits right in.

A wider approach

Fashion Entertainments is a spin-off from Sony's internal innovation program, Seed Acceleration, which is designed to bolster business creation, based on the creative talent and knowledge-base within Sony. The program was formed early in 2014, and is under the direct control of Sony's President and CEO, Kazuo Hirai.

Another interesting project from the Seed Acceleration pipeline is the creative technology platform, MESH (Make, Experience, SHare). MESH is a do-it-yourself platform for creating interconnected wireless hubs for fun and functionality. The idea behind the platform is that you don't have to be an engineer to create wireless information structure, and you don't have to be a programmer to implement it. According to MESH Project Leader at Sony, Takehiro Hagiwara, the applications will span from integrating MESH into anything from toys to smart-home functions. Whatever the users can imagine.

This *open* approach to product innovation resonates on the company's website as well. The MESH team has made an open call for ideas to develop the platform further. This approach is also mimicked on a MESH crowdfunding campaign, which is live as we are writing this. While the FES e-paper watch campaign kept Sony's association hidden, the MESH campaign displays its connection to the Sony Seed Acceleration Program clearly. MESH is positioned as an entrepreneurial venture, but it is 100 percent owned by Sony—everything from manufacturing to usage of intellectual property, delivery, and the risk-assessment at the end of the campaign pitch.

The challenge for a large corporation like Sony is to strike the balance between brand exposure (associated with hiding from the spotlight) and leveraging an increase in customer interest and participation in product development. As we write, the best guess is that transparency will be the only avenue that Sony can take in order to keep projects like the e-paper watch and MESH resonating with the crowds.

One of the key motivating factors for crowdfunders is a sense of urgency. This is where Sony's long-term challenge lies. Where is the urgency in a campaign run by five engineers hired by Sony to (more or less) be "entrepreneurial" and raise funds that would previously be provided by Sony itself? How will Sony communicate that without financial commitment to signal market interest and no product innovation? This is what we have to look out for in years to come as corporate innovation taps into the wisdom of the crowd.

ABN AMRO

Dan Marom and Kevin Berg Grell

The concept of crowdfunding is still viewed by many as a disruptive, independent alternative to traditional finance mechanisms, such as banks and venture capital. Though online platforms have existed for almost a decade, and crowdfunding as a basic concept predates the Internet by thousands of years, it is only in the last few years that the notion of crowdfunding has begun to take hold as anything more than a fringe activity or an odd novelty. That's why it may be somewhat surprising to learn that ABN AMRO, a major financial institution, began working on a plan to incorporate crowdfunding into the array of services it offers, as early as 2009. Dialogue Incubator, ABN AMRO's research branch, eventually launched its crowdfunding platform, Seeds.nl, on May 2012.

The goal was to create an intermediary mechanism that would help connect its entrepreneurial clients with other clients looking for a good investment. And while financial success was always going to be a key element, the people at ABN AMRO realized that the average investor cared about more than just money.

Managing Director of Seeds.nl, Arthur van de Graaf, explains: "Crowdfunding should be more than just profit optimization. We use the term 'personal return of investment,' being a combination of return on involvement, return on investment, and other motivations to invest."

Not one to take a blind leap, however, the cautious nature of a corporate financial institution was revealed when ABN AMRO spent the next few years carefully researching different aspects of crowdfunding. "We did a lot of research and planning to make sure we would launch the right proposition. For instance we investigated what concerns people have when participating in crowdfunding, and designed our proposition such that we resolve all these," says van de Graaf.

Eventually, after careful research and preparation, the company launched Seeds.nl with a pilot of five participating companies. The goal was to facilitate investments in companies with an environmental or social agenda, with the first five companies selected not only because they could benefit from this funding method, but because they could also offer a benefit to society. The companies were:

GreenGraffiti
Offering green, sustainable advertising solutions, which they refer to as "natural media," such as reverse graffiti, sandprinting, moss graffiti, and milk paint

GreenJoy
A boat rental company committed to green transportation and sustainable energy-based vehicles

We Beat the Mountain
Offering recycling solutions for organizations in order to reduce reliance on virgin materials

YUNO
Promoting healthy living by offering healthy, nutritious alternatives to popular children's snacks

Butch and Sundance Media
A company that aims to create a more peaceful society through gaming and storytelling concepts

The initial campaign lasted four months, during which time ABN AMRO funneled investors to the projects through the Seeds platform. The minimum investment amount was €50 ($57), with the goals for most of the projects ranging up to €50,000 ($57,000). The campaigns used several incentives to lure investors. First there were "karmic rewards"—the gratitude of the recipient and the knowledge of helping a good cause. Second there were perks—products or services provided as they become available based on successful funding. Finally there was profit sharing—under certain conditions and if sufficient revenue has been generated, investors received a share of the profits, up to 150 percent of the total investment.

In addition to facilitating a financial quid pro quo, the overall goal of this initiative was to create a long-term relationship between the entrepreneur and investor in the hopes of making crowdfunding sustainable in the long run. "That is typical for banking," notes van de Graaf, "we think in terms of relations rather than transactions."

Campaign results

After the initial campaign three of the five companies met their funding goals: €30,000 ($34,000) for GreenGraffiti; €20,000 ($23,000) for GreenJoy; €35,000 ($40,000) for YUNO. However, while this was a welcome outcome, ABN AMRO did not define the overall success of the initiative as the successful funding of all, or even most, of the projects. "Our own criteria for success of crowdfunding is not that 100 percent of the ideas get funded," says van de Graaf; "it is up to the crowd if entrepreneurs get funded or not."

What made the pilot round of Seeds.nl successful for ABN AMRO was the participation and commitment that it generated from the public. The program was therefore continued with some minor changes, such as the minimum investment amount being lowered to €10 ($11). It is now in its third year and has successfully funded four more start-ups.

Conclusion

The Seeds.nl platform is a groundbreaking success, not because of a unique take on the crowdfunding mechanism (their rewards system is far from being unprecedented), and not because of the great volume of the transactions (they are not going to be posing a threat to Kickstarter anytime soon). Rather, it is their ability to incorporate this new collaborative method of funding into what would otherwise be considered a stronghold of traditional finance. "What we offer is an alternative form of financing in addition to traditional bank loans, angel investors, and other traditional forms of financing," says van de Graaf. "With Seeds.nl we do not want to compete with existing forms of finance, but rather want to complement these."

It is a combination of funding methods that carries significant potential. A financial institution such as ABN AMRO receives thousands of loan requests each year, but many must be turned down because they cannot be justified from a risk/benefit standpoint. However, a forward-thinking bank might benefit from facilitating a collaboration where the risk is shared by many; ideas that might otherwise be discarded could be successfully funded. In addition, the bank could offer its clients a wider range of investment options that aren't available to its competitors. ABN AMRO appears to be that sort of forward-thinking bank. Perhaps others will follow suit.

GE VENTURES AND OURCROWD

Zack Miller, OurCrowd

It's an exciting time to be a start-up investor. We read in the newspaper every day about young companies, fresh with venture funding, growing exponentially, disrupting their industries, and exiting for huge multiples. It's not only angel investors and venture capital (VC) firms seeding the next generation of Ciscos, Akamais, and Oracles. Corporate venture capital firms have also been playing an increasingly important role in the investment landscape. Many large multinationals earmark funds to wholly-owned investment arms to invest in up-and-coming companies. We're accustomed to hearing about Cisco and Samsung making strategic investments but even companies like Walgreens and 7-Eleven have their own VC arms.

To put this in perspective, corporate VCs accounted for $12.31 billion in 656 deals during 2014, a banner year for VC investments in general. Corporate VCs write bigger checks than independent VCs (the average deal size for corporates in 2014 was $23 million, two times that of independents) and those checks are getting bigger (average corporate VC deals in 2013 were around $17 million). While corporate VCs do play an important role, they are still relatively small in the scheme of things (18 percent of total deals are completed by corporate VCs).

Corporate venture capital arms participate in early-stage

investing for two reasons. The first is to make a financial return. Corporates are buying low and selling high when they invest in early-stage technology companies. This can provide a good use of long-term funds for a company, especially ones that throw off a lot of cash. Early-stage investment returns, as measured by the Kauffman Foundation's *Returns to Angel Investors in Groups,* have averaged 27 percent Internal Rate of Return over the long term. Corporates with asset allocation plans understand the risk-return premium and use this asset class to deploy their own cash.

The second reason is to establish an alternative to home-grown R&D. Innovative firms invest heavily in their own R&D arms. This is a clear priority for many of today's top firms, but it doesn't make sense to carry out all R&D in-house. Corporate venture investing enables firms to bet on trends or themes that may not be core to a firm's own skill-set. It seeds external, innovative teams with the necessary capital to execute on their plans to create disruptive and transformative technology. In this way, corporate venture capital complements existing R&D programs.

Many times, corporate investors participate in venture funding as a way to jumpstart innovation. Large innovative firms are great at providing solutions at scale to large problems. Start-ups, on the other hand, have the flexibility and nimbleness to move quickly into a space with a technology solution— without the burden of history or managing thousands of employees or communicating with public shareholders.

With innovation, it's the classic *build vs. buy* decision. Companies need to innovate to stay competitive—it's just a question of how to do that. Corporate venture investing enables a company to do both. Investing in successful start-ups ensures large companies will have full pipelines of next-generation technologies to succeed their own legacy products.

Enter crowdfunding: taking corporate investing to another level

In this era of online investing, corporate investors can use equity crowdfunding to gain access to thousands of compelling, early-stage investment opportunities. Equity crowdfunding platforms, like that of my firm, OurCrowd, aggregate capital from various entities and invest in game-changing start-ups.

Corporate investors, like the venture capital arm of General Electric (GE), GE Ventures, are partnering with equity crowdfunding platforms to supplement their own deal-flow pipelines and access earlier stage investments than they're typically used to seeing. It's an approach that solves a lot of issues for corporate investors looking to maintain an innovative edge:

Crowdfunding scales deal flow

Crowdfunding platforms like OurCrowd see a tremendous amount of deal flow. For example, on a typical month, OurCrowd, which provides due diligence on all the opportunities that appear on its website and invests its own capital alongside that of the "crowd," sees 100–150 business plans every month and ultimately, invests in five of them a month—*every* month. This provides an opportunity for corporate investors to see a broad spectrum of investment opportunities—without having to invest more in building out the internal human capital required to do the same.

Crowdfunding provides differentiated deal flow

Corporate investors can join equity crowdfunding platforms to enter a world of deal flow that's different from what they normally consider. Corporate investors, because they're used to writing big checks, frequently invest in companies seeking growth capital. It's hard to make a case for investing in Series A's when it's too expensive to build deal flow targeting companies raising smaller amounts of money. With crowdfunding, corporates now have the opportunity to invest in companies that previously flew under the radar—in some cases because they're in a slightly different industry, in others because they are at a different point along their maturity cycle.

Corporate investors retain discretion with crowdfunding

Unlike writing a check to an early-stage venture capital firm where an investor loses discretion, equity crowdfunding enables a corporate investor to retain discretion over the investment decision and sit back and wait for the right pitch before swinging. The corporate investors on OurCrowd, for example, conduct their own due diligence alongside the research materials, presentations, and documentation that the platform provides. So they only invest in the opportunities that pass their own investment checklist.

Equity crowdfunding is therefore a powerful option for corporate investors who have existing investment arms or ones that approach investing more opportunistically. It's still early days in the industry and corporate investors are just learning about what makes for best practice when using an equity crowdfunding platform to invest in early-stage companies. As one of the world's largest firms, GE is well-respected for its ability to continuously innovate by developing and investing in new technology. It is now one of the first corporate investors to partner with an equity crowdfunding platform (OurCrowd).

Creating a successful crowdfunding partnership

GE is not only one of the largest companies in the world in terms of market cap (over $250 billion) and number of employees (307,000), but historically, it has also been one of the most innovative. According to the Global Innovation 1000 Study conducted by Strategy&, GE ranked sixth globally in innovation, spending close to $5 billion yearly on research and development. The company, which refers to itself as "the world's oldest start-up" has been the subject of numerous studies and books, citing the firm as a perennial leader in global innovation.

In addition to employing top technology and engineering talent around the world, GE has used various cutting-edge ways to foster innovation both within—and outside—its organization. Early in 2013, OurCrowd began discussions with GE Ventures on a potential collaboration. An agreement was eventually signed in November of 2013, making GE the first of our corporate partners to sign a co-investment agreement and the first corporate investor to tap into crowdfunding. Through this collaboration, the company has the right to co-invest with OurCrowd in select early-stage companies from Israel and to participate globally in the areas of energy, healthcare, software, and advanced manufacturing.

GE Ventures made its first investment on the OurCrowd platform in an interesting start-up, MedAware. According to MedAware, in the U.S. alone, medication errors harm at least 1.5 million people and cause the premature death of more than 220,000 patients annually. Their total cost to the U.S. economy is more than $177 billion each year. The Israeli start-up has set out to reduce each of these figures using software and big data analytics.

This is the first time a Fortune 10 company has invested via an equity crowdfunding company, but it won't be the last. Collaborations of this kind give companies the size of GE investment access to some of the world's most innovative and amazing start-ups.

Best practice for an equity crowdfunding collaboration

Not all equity crowdfunding platforms were created equal and there are certain nuances to understand upfront when you're looking to partner with one. The following are a few important distinctions you'll want to consider when looking at the equity crowdfunding space:

Open vs curated platforms

OurCrowd performs due diligence on all the companies that appear on its platform in a process that's pretty analogous to the research work that venture capitalists do when making an investment. That means a curated group of opportunities for corporate investors and a lighter research burden placed on partners. But it also means that the number of total opportunities will be limited when compared to a platform that does less or no vetting up front. It's important to understand how opportunities make their way onto the equity crowdfunding platform you're looking at because it will affect how much work you'll have to do with your team. You'll have to determine whether you prefer curated deal flow or would rather see more potential deals on your way to making equity crowdfunding investments.

The business model of the equity crowdfunding platform

OurCrowd invests its own capital in each deal, making its money by charging investors on its platform a yearly management fee on the capital deployed and a share of profits. We don't charge the companies who receive an OurCrowd investment. This was done deliberately to position the platform on the same side of the table as its investors—if the companies perform well, everyone wins. OurCrowd also continues to support its portfolio companies after an investment is made, in an effort to help raise the probability of a successful return on investment.

Other platforms have different business models, including some that charge companies a brokerage fee for raising capital. Take time to understand a prospective equity crowdfunding platform's incentives and sources of revenue. This influences the nature of the deal flow you'll see and the role the platform plays in the lifecycle of your investment.

Lead investor or follower

At OurCrowd we both lead deals and will participate in a round led by a top venture capital firm. In the case of leading a deal, it's likely that we will receive a board seat in return for our investment (the same isn't necessarily true when another venture capital firm acts as the lead investor). We can then place experienced professionals on to the boards of the start-ups we invest in to represent our interests and those of our investors. Other platforms take a different stance to leading deals. Always ask an equity crowdfunding platform about their approach to leading deals and taking an active role in corporate governance to ensure it works with your model.

Frequency of deals and total deal cycle time

At this stage, OurCrowd invests in five opportunities, plus or minus, every month. As a corporate investor, that volume may be pretty aggressive. Additionally, some of the investments OurCrowd makes can fill up in a matter of days. Closing times are quick; OurCrowd can launch and close an investment round in a matter of weeks. Corporate investors like GE can move fast but this pace can be quick even for one of the world's most innovative companies.

One of the things we have learned in partnership with GE is that this volume and quick deal cycle time requires special attention from both parties. OurCrowd now gives GE an early heads-up when it's launching a new investment, providing a jumpstart to GE Ventures' research process. When working on standard operating procedures with an equity crowdfunding partner, be sure to talk about the funding and closing process of the investments. As a corporate investor, you may need some added time on both ends of the deal—the diligence and closing processes. A good partner can create a real-life, workable process to incorporate your own firm's needs.

Setting a point person on both sides of the relationship

To establish a working partnership, GE spent time engaging in lots of discussion and conducting serious due diligence on OurCrowd, its team, and its process. The success of the collaboration is due in part to the fact that both parties established point people: executives who were both incentivized to get the partnership done and had the corporate clout to help see it through.

Appointing key team members is really important in the partnership process as likely, there will be many different people participating in the process at different points in time. These point people will also serve as project managers to help shepherd the negotiations through and ensure that once launched, both parties find a way to continue to tweak the relationship for maximum success.

Getting the full PR value out of the relationship

After a corporate investor/crowdfunding platform partnership is signed, both parties are going to want to let their constituencies know about the value in the relationship. This has deep branding implications that can affect both sides of the agreement. For the corporate investor, it shows a commitment to innovation and technology advancement, as well as creative allocation of investment capital. For the equity crowdfunding platform, having corporate investors participating on the platform is a big credibility boost to existing and new investors on the platform, as well as to prospective corporate investors.

At OurCrowd we coordinated with GE's corporate communications department to approve the messaging and branding in the PR. A day was set for the announcement to go out and the PR arms of both firms spoke to the press about this groundbreaking collaboration, resulting in redistribution, hundreds of social media shares, and thousands of page-views.

Like most partnerships, getting an agreement signed gets you just part of the way toward the finish line. What happens after signing a partnership can be as important, if not more important, than the original paperwork in terms of reaching the partnership's initial objectives. As a corporate investor, here are a few things you can do once you sign a partnership with an equity crowdfunding platform to optimize for success:

Hold regular progress calls

To keep the communication channels open, it's a good idea to have regular progress calls between partners. These calls are really good to talk about open issues that haven't been resolved and to plan for the future. For example, it became clearer to OurCrowd as the GE relationship matured that the corporate investor could benefit from added cycle time both before the deal was launched and during the closing period. The equity crowdfunding platform obliged, tweaking its process along the way.

Participate in each other's events

Equity crowdfunding is still in its early days and growth is tremendous. Frequently, platforms like OurCrowd take their portfolio companies on the road and corporate investors should take advantage of these events to meet both with the platform's senior management but also with the entrepreneurs receiving an investment. These events help to make real the world of virtual, online investing and there's little substitute to seeing a good entrepreneur give his elevator pitch. These events are also good to see and hear other investors and their questions and feedback on prospective investment opportunities.

Communicate investment parameters
It may sound self-explanatory but it's important for corporate investors to give continuous feedback on the investment candidates it's reviewing on the equity crowdfunding platform. That way, the platform can work to identify opportunities that best fit the corporate investor's mandate. This can certainly impact the industries that appear on the equity crowdfunding platform but also the corporate maturities and total deal sizes of the investments available.

Corporate venture investing via equity crowdfunding platforms is just beginning. The ability to identify, perform due diligence, and process the sheer breadth of opportunities online is staggering. But sometimes the pace of deal flow and the speed at which deals are being done can put a strain on corporate investors. Identifying a quality equity crowdfunding platform as a partner will help structure a relationship which can move the innovation needle significantly forward for large corporations by investing in early-stage companies.

IBM

Anna Grosman
and Ana Brandes, Aston University

IBM's crowdfunding efforts can be grouped into two phases. The first "experimental" stage was started on a small scale in 2012 by the IBM Research division and consisted of an internal platform on which employees of the IBM Research division could pitch potential projects and company purchases, addressing both individual and organizational needs. Employees could invest their allocated budgets from corporate funds into one or more proposals on a "spend-it-or-lose-it" basis. They could follow, critique, share or comment on projects as well as suggest improvements. As a result, the crowdfunding platform was used by more employees than other internal collaboration tools at IBM and projects reflecting previously unsatisfied needs and beyond day-to-day assignments were funded.

The second phase started in 2013 when leadership of the enterprise crowdfunding project was transferred to a larger department within IBM—the CIO Organization, which handles internal IT work for IBM. Due to its larger scope, individual budgets (and the total fund) were increased, but investments were limited to software and technology-related projects. In 2014 enterprise crowdfunding was opened to the whole of IBM, and this time the theme was limited to mobile applications. Employee engagement and cross-departmental collaboration increased, and a variety of successfully funded projects demonstrated employee innovation and entrepreneurship. The investment decision-making process was considerably improved, with employees seeing their projects through from origination to deployment in a much shorter period of time.

IBM has been setting the pace for technological innovation since 1945. Its history includes five Nobel prizes and the most U.S. patents that any company has held for the past twenty years. Today it has the broadest range of patented technologies in the industry. Since 1998, IBM has also been at the forefront of open-source innovation and crowdsourcing, working with collaborative communities on the development of its Linux operating system and software products. In addition to its crowdsourcing engagement, IBM has been testing innovative systems for employee-initiated contributions since 2005, and its first crowdfunding project—the 1×5 project—was duly deployed in 2012.

1×5 project

IBM's 1×5 project was one of the world's first enterprise crowdfunding projects. For the purposes of its first trial run, a time limit of thirty-five days was imposed based on research suggesting that shorter durations encourage focus and a sense of urgency in large-scale inter-organizational collaborations (Millen and Fontaine, 2003). According to Michael Muller, an ACM Distinguished Scientist at IBM Research, the idea for this platform was originated when a Research Vice-President at IBM decided to reinvigorate the innovation culture. It was for this purpose that IBM

Research set up an internal platform on which employees could pitch potential projects and company purchases, addressing both individual and organizational needs. A total of 511 employees were included in the first phase of the project. They received a fixed budget of $100 per person, which they could invest in one or more proposals by other employees on a "spend-it-or-lose-it" basis. Projects ranged from the purchase of an office 3D printer to hosting a lecture series.

Furthermore, employees could follow, critique, share, or comment on the projects as well as suggest improvements. Some proposers, or "ideators," offered rewards to investors, such as priority usage of the future resource. They were also allowed to enlist teams of IBMers who volunteered their expertise and time to help develop the crowdfunded projects. Participation in the project as a whole was entirely voluntary. At the start and throughout the trial, the Vice President of the sponsoring department (which provided corporate funds) sent frequent announcements on the progress of the crowdfunding campaign—a form of communication by top leadership that proved to be important.

The 1×5 project successfully reached its goal of employee-generated innovation. The headline outcomes were:

Higher employee participation than in other social media applications

A total of 48 percent of employees from the sponsoring department took part in the project and nineteen proposals (or 56 percent of projects) were successfully funded. This compares to a 40 percent success rate at Kickstarter, 13 percent in the most active online communities of IBM, and 10 percent participation in social media applications. Some 32 percent of the available funds were awarded to the nineteen successful projects.

Proposals addressed diverse individual and organizational needs and involved extensive interdepartmental collaboration

In general, proposals related to such employee needs as new and challenging technologies, resources needed to work, and extensions of cultures of experimentation and morale boosters. The project gave employees a greater voice in the innovation process, supported interdepartmental collaboration, and brought people together to meet their shared needs. Proposers reported that 42 percent of support for their individual projects came from employees unknown to them.

According to Michael Muller, who ran both trials for the 1×5 project, "Groups came together finding out that they had the same needs and launched projects together. People started working together for mutual success. Even when two projects were funded in the same area, employees started working together instead of against each other. And in the end both projects got funded. Employees with successfully funded projects benefited by doing good and by speeding up their careers." Overall, the 1×5 project facilitated decision-making processes regarding investments, which were traditionally characterized by a long set of approvals and some bureaucracy.

Funded projects reflected previously unsatisfied needs and needs beyond day-to-day assignments
Employees appeared to use the 1×5 project to get resources that served the specific needs of disciplines non-core to their organization where funding was more difficult to get through traditional methods. For example, most funded (and pitched) projects were in the categories of equipment (3D printer, robotics, sports equipment), Internet accounts (micro-tasking tools, surveys), and morale-boosters (i.e. beverages).

Another motivation for funding the projects lay in the pursuit of particular technological interests that did not coincide with the main assignments of employees. Such proposals were creative (robotics) or contributed to the development of knowledge that would be valuable in the future (3D printer).

Innovative promotion strategies by proposers to potential investors seemed to play an important role. The overall success was due to concretizing the innovation process around monetary contributions and change in employees' workplaces, as well as opportunity to join forces with others around topics initiated by employees themselves.

iFundIT project overview
The success of the 1×5 project caught the interest of IBM's CIO Organization, a 6,000 employee division that handles

internal IT for IBM. The CIO division seemed an appropriate fit for enterprise crowdfunding as it was strongly virtualized and decentralized, with some employees working entirely from home. The 1×5 project was a new technology and enabled innovation on a much broader scale and hence appealed to the core purpose of the CIO organization, which was aimed at fostering employee collaboration and innovation. The 1×5 software tool was changed slightly to adapt it to a larger organization. Françoise LeGoues, the former Vice-President for Innovation in the CIO Organization who was leading this initiative, recalls that she was initially skeptical of this new experiment and was not aware of any firm outside IBM experimenting with enterprise crowdfunding—but the project ended up being a total success.

The 2013 trial at the IT department had a larger scope, was focused entirely on software and technology, and was thought of as a replacement to traditional methods of innovation. In due course the project was rebranded to the unequivocal name of iFundIT. Again, participation was voluntary and opt-in. A total of 302 employees registered and received a personal budget of $2,000 each.

In 2014, participation was opened up to the whole of IBM, but the theme was limited to mobile applications; an increasing proportion of employees relied on mobile phones to do their jobs, while there was a clear shortage of mobile apps that could be used to facilitate their daily tasks. To match this need, the CIO organization invested a considerable share of its 2014 IT budget with the goal of giving all 400,000 IBM employees the chance to become an "ideator" or an investor. From June to November 2014, 6,000 employees from thirty-five countries registered as investors. The successful investors were given a further $2,000 to their initial $2,000 investment budget. A total of 150 ideas were fully funded and moved forward for implementation.

According to Barbara Mathers, Vice President, CIOLab, IBM Office of the CIO, who was in charge of the two latest campaigns in 2014, three major adjustments were made to iFundIT relative to previous versions: 1) the scale of the tool was further expanded to handle the volume, 2) the ideator- and investor-experience was improved and 3) a larger execution team was put in place, which handled and maintained the tool and executed the projects once they were successfully funded. Multiple iFundIT rounds resulted in a number of successfully funded projects; there were about a dozen projects from the 2013 iFundIT trials and half a dozen from the 2014 rounds deployed as of November 2014. Ideators could be split into three distinct categories 1) technical, i.e. they could contribute to subsequent coding of the project, 2) non-technical but very familiar with the context in which the app was required, and 3) the "inbetweeners" or "power users" of mobile devices but with no specific coding skills. It is the first category of technically skilled ideators that IBM wanted to involve further in the implementation of successful projects.

Notable among the successfully financed projects was IBM Client Experience, a mobile app that allows employees to build a mock-up solution during a client meeting, as an alternative to PowerPoint. There were also some applications potentially suitable for commercialization such as the Blue Dial Tag—a way of tagging business calls as opposed to personal calls on a mobile bill, which allowed users to itemize the bill before expensing it.

The iFundIT enterprise crowdfunding project has again proven to be a success. Its major outcomes were:

Employees were motivated to participate for social rather than financial reasons

According to Françoise LeGoues who ran the project during 2013: "The biggest impact so far has been cultural. People love it, because it makes their jobs more fun and gives them a chance to invent solutions for business problems that have been frustrating them."

Barbara Mathers, in charge of the 2014 campaigns, reflected on the beneficial changes brought about the project: "iFundIT empowers employees to become entrepreneurs inside the company; it gives them the chance to contribute and receive the recognition they deserve. Enterprise crowdfunding increases employee engagement and collaboration. It increases employee power and flips the innovation-decision process upside down… enterprise crowdfunding allows you to shorten the decision-making process significantly and gives employees an instant gratification of seeing their projects from origination to deployment in a much shorter period of time."

The employees were not the only ones to benefit directly from iFundIT. As Françoise LeGoues recalled, the organization as a whole also reaped the fruits of crowd-funding: "Very often the employees thought that if we'd funded that technology, a lot of IBMers would use it and the CIO organization would look better. It was not necessarily for a profit but more because it would improve the reputation of the CIO organization and IBM."

Regarding the two iFundIT campaigns that ran across the whole of IBM in 2014, Barbara Mathers added: "The mobile apps make the employees' work easier and some even accomplish a specific business goal. Therefore employee effectiveness rose as a result of iFundIT, of which IBM directly benefited."

The iFundIT project generated a number of benefits for IBM. Participation rose with each conducted round. Employees appreciated having control over their decisions and over how their workplace was orchestrated. It represented a clear departure from the classic innovation-decision process and an improvement in employee-led innovation at IBM. It is now easier and faster for an employee to get their idea heard and to actually execute it. Employees also identified themselves with IBM, which improved corporate loyalty. It was easy to draw similarities between the crowdfunding initiative and IBM's corporate venture capital activities, as Françoise LeGoues explained: "All of the projects are intended to improve the way we do things internally. They address a variety of issues, from making the supply chain more efficient, to better sales tools, to internal apps for different uses."

Distance-related frictions were diminished

There was a small increase in probability that someone would fund a project if he or she was from the same country, culture, or division as the employee launching the project. However overall employees did cross these boundaries, in the sense of countries and working teams. This reflects the findings of broader research conducted by Agrawal et al. (2011), which concluded that crowdfunding platforms eliminate most distance-related economic frictions normally associated with seed- or early-stage financing. The platforms facilitate the acquisition of information, the monitoring of progress, and the possibilities of providing input. In the case of IBM, enterprise crowdfunding helped to strengthen a common identity and diminish departmental borders.

Successful projects addressed collective concerns at multiple levels of the organization

The project showed that there was slightly more benefit for employees at mid-management and operational levels. iFundIT changed the typical top-down decision-making process, where projects were approved by a review board. This speeded development up and projects were launched in a matter of weeks instead of months.

In the iFundIT project, about 70 percent of backers were originally unknown to proposers, although the former were able to access personal profile information about the latter. This suggests that employees were mostly pursuing organizational or commercial needs, as projects often focused on improving the organizational environment and investment decisions reflected previously unsatisfied needs.

Inclusive innovation

According to Françoise LeGoues, corporate crowdfunding involved people who previously did not contribute to innovation. The organization has previously run project contests but not all employees participated. About ten projects were typically submitted following the launch of a contest, with a total of only fifty employees involved across all projects. In the crowdfunding campaign of 2013, all 6,000 employees of the CIO organization were told that they could register as investors and be allocated money, so that they could all fund innovation—a more than ten-fold increase in participation.

Limitations and implementation issues

The CIO organization has identified some issues to address before it runs its next enterprise crowdfunding campaign. Firstly, there was an upper limit on the number of investors, resulting in some employees not being able to register. Secondly, registered investors often did not spend all their budgets. Thirdly, the ideators or investors did not typically get involved in the actual deployment of projects. Unlike in traditional equity or reward-based crowdfunding, the implementation was handled by the IBM execution team. One way to increase investor and ideator participation in the implementation process would be for IBM to use a reward scheme. However, it is hard to calculate the appropriate level of monetary reward for successful ideators and investors based on the incremental financial returns of the crowdfunded projects. An alternative would be for IBM to encourage ideators to include non-monetary rewards for investors more systematically in their projects. Finally, the employees did not get free time for proposing projects or investing. Any engagement by an employee in enterprise crowdfunding and conducting projects had to happen in addition to their usual workload, hence not everyone decided to participate.

IBM is a highly decentralized IT company at which most of the work is matrixed and virtualized. The question is whether enterprises with other organizational cultures or structures could benefit as much from enterprise crowdfunding as IBM did. However, according to both Barbara Mathers and Françoise LeGoues, it wasn't the structure that was important but the type of employees—i.e. people willing to engage and try "new cool things." They believe the process could be successfully deployed in any type of organization with a similar culture, especially for large companies where crowdfunding is perhaps the only way to achieve inclusive innovation. On this basis, enterprise crowdfunding might work just as well in a non-tech environment such as Walmart or McDonald's, where employees like to be engaged and appreciate the chance to make a difference.

There is much to be learned from the way in which IBM has used crowdfunding as a new way to communicate and innovate inside the company. Many of the funded projects succeeded and resulted in immediate benefits for IBM. They often began as internal tools which boosted the firm's own efficiency, but they could also be sold later on as corporate products. Hence IBM might one day commercialize its crowdfunding platform and offer services to its clients as a white label.

By allowing any of its employees to be an innovator and creating a mechanism to push new ideas through to implementation, IBM has delivered a significant boost both to its level of innovation and to employee morale. Enterprise crowdfunding has proved to be a unique way for a large organization such as IBM to support small innovative projects.

4

CROWDFUNDING AND CORPORATE SOCIAL RESPONSIBILITY

Kevin Berg Grell and Dan Marom

It has long been judged important for businesses to contribute to the quality of life of their workforce, the local community, and society at large. It was once enough for a business to demonstrate its "Corporate Social Responsibility" by writing out checks to a local charity, but today CSR has become a key aspect of the way a business conducts itself. In an ever-competitive free market environment, CSR strategy is quickly becoming a way for an enterprise to differentiate itself from its competitors, acquire and retain customers, and engage with its employees and stakeholders. An effective CSR department within a company can in fact be as important as product development and traditional marketing in customer acquisition and loyalty.

The premise for CSR initiatives is that business decisions should not only take into account government regulation and short-term financial gains, but also long-term impact on the sustainability of the company (relationships with stakeholders, resources, etc.) and the environment in which it operates. As the World Business Council for Sustainable Development puts it: "As an engine for social progress, CSR helps companies live up to their responsibilities as global citizens and local neighbors in a fast-changing world. And acting in a socially responsible manner is more than just an ethical duty for a company, but is something that actually has a bottom line pay-off." (WBCSD 1)

The challenge of CSR

Corporations have now started using crowdfunding mechanisms to improve the way in which they measure, evaluate, and communicate their CSR efforts, thereby engaging more effectively with their customers, employees, and stakeholders. In an age of increasing ethical consumerism, customers want to know about the nature and impact of a company's CSR initiatives. Shareholders also want to know where their money is going, and employees want to be involved in the good works of their organization. Traditional methods of communication, such as annual reports and PR/media pushes don't foster the same level of transparency and visibility that crowdfunding does, and crucially they don't allow for that communication to be a two-way process. As Marc Benioff, Chairman and CEO of Salesforce.com, puts it: "We plan to follow our people, and … invest in what our people are passionate about."

Crowdfunding transforms CSR into a collaborative, reward-based, and performance-driven process. It is integrated, diversified, scalable, and global. CSR in corporations becomes incentivized, both internally and externally, providing active engagement for employees and customers alike. Where traditional CSR reporting is often unclear and seen as self-promotion, crowdfunding mechanisms offer real-time data streams of performance and change, which are viewed as transparent and collaborative.

Where traditional CSR initiatives were selected and directed by executive management, today they can follow the ideals and opinion of the crowd. Interaction with stakeholders through CSR crowdfunding networks provides details of people and their priorities and can help predict opportunities—a huge competitive advantage in many industries.

CEO Paul Polman from Unilever provides a great example: "We missed the issue of obesity and the value of healthy and nutritional food. We were behind, while Nestlé was riding that wave. Not being in tune with society, with the benefit of hindsight, can cost you dearly." With improved engagement on social issues, an enterprise will be in much better position to foresee changes in the landscape.

CSR and crowdfunding

So how does crowdfunding have a meaningful impact on a company's CSR efforts? Essentially it works by opening up the corporation's internal strategic direction to the public and making them partners in the corporation's efforts. Crowdfunding campaigns, hosted by a corporation as a customer-facing tool, can be posted directly on a company's website or through an existing platform. Partnering with a charitable organization trying to raise $1 million, for example, a company could promise to match all donations if the campaign reaches the $500,000 threshold. The effects of an initiative like this are twofold: the company escapes the self-promotion of their philanthropic activities and it receives positive PR and marketing through the evangelical supporters of a cause; essentially, they become the hero of the crowd team's efforts for half the cost.

The company also becomes engrained in the campaign and in the donor experience via messages and alerts or updates on the success and impact of the campaign and the company's involvement in it. There are multiple options for a company to embed itself in a CSR crowdfunding initiative

141.

in this way: examples include donations made to a specific campaign, support in covering sponsor fees, or perks pledged for donors. As visibility grows with the reach of all involved parties (the company, the charity or cause, the supporting public), dollars raised similarly increase. Viral tendencies online indicate that the more attention and support a movement garners, the more people want to jump in and get involved.

The social responsibility of a corporation deals as much with its own people as it does with the community. Just as companies can set up internal crowdfunding to incite innovation, employees can be encouraged to spearhead campaigns to support a co-worker or a cause directly related to the business and its activities. Mechanisms such as these connect and bond an organization and create a very strong corporate culture.

Internal or external, CSR crowdfunding mechanisms create a strong link between the enterprise and the people— one that is open, transparent, and where both sides feel that they are on the same team in the pursuit of social progress. Such methods can also accomplish much more than simply raising money. One way this is possible is through the validation of project ideas and gauging of support from the public. As part of a campaign, a corporation can solicit ideas or solutions to social challenges through the crowd. The crowd feels involved in the process, and the corporation then spearheads the crowdsourced innovation. This way, the projects become a community decision, and together all stakeholders crowdfund the budget for a project. It allows corporations to identify a change of importance to both the business and society, and to champion an innovative proof-of-concept solution that it can then hand over to government or a foundation. This approach benefits all parties: the company does not need to remain involved over time, and the government and other stakeholders benefit from suggested solutions. Further, all parties share in the ultimate benefit: an improvement in the social issue originally targeted.

Verizon's Ivan Seidenberg explains: "Our belief is that corporate philanthropy expands the business. If you do the right thing over time, you expand the capabilities of your customer base, business, and society." Sharing his own positive experience, Aetna's Chairman and CEO Ron Williams says, "Through philanthropy, we can help develop new models and programs that can be brought to scale by the government."

Implications

According to a recent McKinsey survey, 95 percent of CEOs feels that society now has higher expectations of businesses taking on public responsibilities than it did five years ago. This provides an incredible opportunity for enterprises to become powerful voices of the people, and in so doing extend their loyal stakeholders far beyond the employees that work for them.

According to the 2013 Cone Communications/Echo Global CSR Study, more than eight-in-ten consider CSR when deciding where to work (81 percent), what to buy or where to shop (87 percent) and which products and services to recommend to others (85 percent). These new, socially conscious consumers use their purchasing power to create impact and promote change. In the past year, for example, 70 percent of millennials have purchased a product that supports a cause. Furthermore, they will switch brands in order to support a cause; an overwhelming 89 percent are likely to switch from one brand to another (if price and quality are equal) if the second supports a cause.

Both customers and employees demand a socially responsible business, and the social missions of an organization now play a huge role in the competitive recruitment of talented employees. Highly sought after millennials are increasingly more selective about the values of the companies they choose to work for and an internal system of CSR crowdfunding can create a very desirable environment. As Mike Kelly, head of CSR at KPMG Europe, puts it: "Ask almost any large company about the business rationale for its CSR efforts and you will be told that they help to motivate, attract, and retain staff. People want to work at a company where they share the values and the ethos."

Cause-based consumerism also adds a whole new dimension to the brand of an enterprise. These "cause" brands have a unique competitive advantage over others in their industry, and as we have seen, younger generations are willing to put their money where their mouth is. A product carries with it the identity of the company that makes it, with social responsibility/impact at the heart of the reputation. Look at what TOMS® has done in intertwining their entire business with a global cause, successfully turning every customer into a global philanthropist (see page 157).

Crowdfunding also addresses the challenge of impact evaluation that besets traditional CSR methods. Former Walmart CEO, Mike Duke, corroborates this notion: "There is definitely a need for measurement. Evaluation can be one of the most challenging aspects of engaging in a social and environmental issue, yet if our activities are not measured, they lose their importance." Social issues also evolve over time, making ongoing measurement a clear priority.

As you will see in the case studies that follow, CSR departments are starting to make good use of crowdfunding methods to achieve the kind of impacts discussed here. But this is only the beginning. More and more examples will quickly emerge and innovative strategies will be refined. The CSR crowdfunding revolution has only just begun.

DC ENTERTAINMENT

Robert Lusk, Jr.

In the mid-1980s, West Africa was hit hard by famine. Hundreds of thousands died and millions more were left in extreme poverty. In 1986, DC Entertainment got involved by releasing a comic book titled *Heroes Against Hunger*, with all proceeds donated to the Ethiopian Famine Relief Fund. The initiative had a huge impact in raising awareness and in solidifying DC's image as a responsible enterprise.

In 2012, the region was again faced with famine and millions of people were again in desperate need of help. DC Entertainment, now a subsidiary of Warner Bros., was once more quick to respond. This time, by incorporating the resources and strategies of a crowdfunding campaign, DC's *We Can Be Heroes* project saw remarkable success, uniting employees, fans, and the general public alike. In its first year alone, the campaign raised over $2 million, which was split between three organizations (Mercy Corps, Save the Children, and the International Rescue Committee), which put it to best use on the ground in Africa.

In contrast to the 1986 project (which was a single edition comic to raise money), *We Can Be Heroes* was more advanced in its way of creating social engagement. The company matched employee and consumer donations up to the first million dollars; it released a specialty merchandise line that gave 50 percent of sales to the cause; and it effectively utilized the superheroes brand to promote involvement in the campaign. The Justice League characters—Aquaman, Green Lantern, Superman, Batman, Wonder Woman, The Flash, and Cyborg—became the faces of *We Can Be Heroes*, engaging fans through specific challenges and product lines and providing perks for involvement.

The campaign website—www.WeCanBeHeroes.org— served as a base for all activity and connected all players in the campaign. There, people could make donations, purchase specially branded merchandise, receive newsletters and updates on the current state of affairs in the region of focus, and connect with others in the *We Can Be Heroes* online community. Each of the partner organizations was highlighted and there was a clear connection between the operations of the campaign and the objectives in Africa.

DC also pushed to create exposure and drive traffic. *We Can Be Heroes* was featured in magazines such as *People* and *Sports Illustrated*, as well as a spot on the "Anderson Cooper Show." It received collaborative support from music artist Daughtry, who recorded an acoustic version of his hit song "Rescue Me," with net proceeds from iTunes benefiting the campaign. Daughtry and his band also included the song in concerts on their U.S. "Break the Spell" tour, further spreading the *We Can Be Heroes* message to new audiences.

During the project's second year, with a strong buzz and substantial public awareness, DC turned to Indiegogo for the next stage of its crowdfunding campaign. The Indiegogo-based roll-out featured multiple phases focused on different superheroes, all under the tagline: "Get something good. Do something great." The stages, themed around Batman, Wonder Woman, Superman, and the Justice League itself, had hero-specific perks that were offered to donors at various price levels.

Perk prices ranged from about $10 to $3,000, from t-shirts and sets of signed memorabilia by DC writers and artists to Comic-Con travel packages that included airfare and hotel, passes to the event, and the opportunity to meet DC artists. DC also rolled out special, one-of-a-kind offerings, that ranged up to $25,000. Examples of these perks included the chance to be drawn into a Batman comic and keep the original artwork, a barbecue with DC co-publishers/artists Geoff Johns and Jim Lee for $5,000, and a visit by Jim Lee to paint a custom mural on your wall at home. These crowdfunding campaigns, with thousands of new donors, raised more than $415,000 on their own.

DC Entertainment also partnered with Sharecraft and the Save the Children Challenge in order to bring on board the active online gamer population. The project allowed people to start their own sub-fundraisers, and through the use of live online gaming, it went viral. Led by Athene, a professional gamer and YouTube celebrity, gamers everywhere were invited daily to get involved and rewards and recognition were offered as incentives throughout the community. Over 22,000 gamers participated in the campaign, which linked gamification of superheroes and sub-fundraising campaigns.

Conclusion

The overall campaign proved to be a huge success and a model for DC Entertainment's future CSR efforts. It raised over $2.3 million and helped over five million men, women, and children in the Horn of Africa. The exposure of the initiative reached millions, with collaboration from an array of outlets ranging from national news stations to professional video gamers. It's important to note that DC's consumer market base consists of comic fans that are typically males between the ages of eighteen and thirty-four. This demographic is one of the lowest in terms of charitable contributions, and yet DC was able to incite a passionate following through the connection of the brand's characters with real-life issues.

The success of the campaign validates the collaborative methods of CSR crowdfunding and provides an adjustable template for other bigger initiatives in the future. DC utilized the concept of "glocality" by balancing global scale with local, personal impact (like the individual sub-fundraisers of gamers through Sharecraft and the use of sharing across individual social networks). Individual donations were linked to specific applications of the allotted funds, so that donors knew exactly what was being done with their small contribution. The community, for example, was updated on drought projects as well as long-term solutions that involved training local groups. Sanitation and water-delivery programs, like wells and pipelines, were implemented and reported back to the community in a transparent manner.

DC made particularly effective use of its brand to drive its crowdfunding success, by closely incorporating its Justice League characters and related product perks into the campaign. In a mutually beneficial manner, the brand and the cause became one. The key was to tie the issue and the perks to the popular characters. Comic lovers, comic artists, and the superheroes themselves all teamed up to defeat the famine—another effective example of the power of the crowd.

CSR CROWDFUNDING— A PLATFORM'S PERSPECTIVE

Liz Deering and Mark Courtney, 121Giving

It's been called "cause marketing"—a term familiar to any business executive who has ever written a check in support of a charity, organization, or cause. Usually, the expenditure officially attaches the company name and brand logo to a recognizable and visible event or campaign: a walkathon, a brightly colored wristband, a 5-km race, a lapel pin or satin ribbon, a branded sports car, a fund-raiser, a concert, or the fee for a celebrity spokesperson. In fact, according to sponsorship experts IEG, major brands will soon spend more on causes and corporate social responsibility (CSR) programs than the billions they spend to advertise their own products and services.

But there's a problem. Despite growing investments, many CSR initiatives are neither long-term nor financially sustainable for the companies that sponsor them. Instead, CSR programs have tended to be one-time campaign-oriented or focused on a single cause or event, leaving consumers wondering if corporations and brands really have their hearts in the right places. Are corporations really interested in solving social, environmental, health, and educational problems? Or are they simply looking for another avenue for promoting their brand image? Consumers really do want to know: do companies truly care if anything happens as a result of their donations, sponsorships, and "cause marketing"?

So why is this? Companies have recognized that connecting with consumers on an affinity thread is very smart business. They understand that relationships with consumers are built by creating great value in the shopping aisle *and* by establishing a warmer connection that focuses on "doing well by doing good." Evidence is clear that consumers want to be involved in the good that brands accomplish—but they also expect transparency and a connected experience. In other words, consumers desire more connection between the dollars they give and the impact those dollars make, and they highly favor companies that put their money where their hearts are. In fact, marketing and PR firm Cone Communications has found that 71 percent of Americans want brands to show their "good" by changing their operations, donating products, or advocating to support local causes.

The goal of CSR is a simple yet complex challenge for companies: build emotional loyalty with consumers by demonstrating a commitment to bettering the world. In turn, convert those consumers into customers, and/or retain already-loyal customers. Examining the evolution of crowdfunding as a way to create emotional loyalty with customers provides a framework for examining some of the solutions developed by creative companies who "get it." And we'll offer some strategies to start changing the thinking so that CSR can be done differently—and in a way that uses new tools like crowdfunding to achieve results that match consumers' needs for impact, transparency, and value while also meeting corporations' business goals as they pursue CSR.

What's missing—the CSR landscape now

Before crowdfunding and the technology platforms that enable crowdfunding existed, companies raised or donated money outright for causes. For years, companies have offered cause-focused merchandise and partnered with large non-profits to that end. The original Susan G. Komen Breast Cancer Foundation (now known simply as Susan G. Komen) first introduced the eponymous pink ribbon in the early nineties in a grassroots partnership with Estée Lauder Cosmetics. Other companies, for decades, have relied on consumer reach and/or specialized products to raise funds for causes. And while all these methods have delivered important donations to charities and elevated the visibility of key causes and the brands that participated, an underlying problem also evolved: consumers became much more scrutinizing.

The argument can be made that crowdfunding essentially pioneered itself through CSR initiatives, although it's a challenge to pinpoint exactly when or how it caught on. According to Cause Marketing Forum's 2013 Report, "America's Charity Checkout Champions," sixty national retailers helped raise more than $358 million combined using crowdfunding, $54 million of it directly through campaigns with shoppers on eBay (the site's "Giving Works" program empowers its sellers to earmark a percentage of their sales proceeds to charity, and invites buyers to make contributions as well).

Yet this approach to engagement has inherent challenges. Consumers might not want to donate, for example, to muscular dystrophy or lung cancer research. Perhaps they have an affinity for animals in shelters or helping the homeless instead. As they do with other services, consumers increasingly expect options and choice when they give to charity. According to IEG, since 2009 there has been a growing trend toward consumers having more control of where their cause marketing dollars are spent. By way of proof, the "Millennial Impact, 2013" report from research agency Achieve says that 70 percent of millennials are willing to raise money on behalf of a nonprofit they care about.

Often, however, consumers can feel obligated or even coerced into giving—especially at the checkout. Despite the rise of so-called transactional giving models, consumers are likely not in an ideal psychological or altruistic state to give when they are shopping, and cash-register solicitation often leads to a poor brand experience. It's therefore debatable whether this form of giving actually provides a positive differentiator for the cause-supporting brand—one that is supposed to boost image perception—given how commoditized and forced it has become.

Another problem is that many CSR initiatives are short-term in nature—which often comes with short-term impressions and results. A retailer, for example, might sponsor a campaign on behalf of a partner charity and raise significant money annually. Consumers might make the correlation that a company cares about a certain affinity but then struggle to connect the CSR campaign with a tangible, overall impact—a key detriment of short-lived campaign-based strategies.

On the flip side, campaigning with long-term charity partners can achieve a significant amount of good will, impact, and financial reward while creating a more lasting customer impression. One example is Kmart's partnership with March of Dimes. Since 1983, the organization has raised $103 million through customer campaigns, illustrating that a long-term partnership can drive increased consumer loyalty for a brand over time.

But increased consumer scrutiny has also arisen with these campaigns. According to Giving USA, individuals gave $335 billion while corporations gave $16 billion in 2013—numbers that are repeatedly presented by socially conscious consumers to illustrate the need for brands to do better at matching customers' interests in giving. According to Cone Communications in its 2013 Social Impact Study: "As consumers become increasingly sophisticated about the role corporations can play in society, companies must aspire to meet equally high and diverse expectations. Simply writing a check isn't going to cut it. Companies must consider the impact they want to have, and the best way to achieve it—and often that means a multi-faceted approach."

Capturing emotional loyalty through basic crowdfunding

In a limited sense, businesses have been using crowdfunding as part of their CSR activities for quite some time, insofar as they have set up projects that are then contributed to and funded by their customers. Some representative examples include:

Coffee Bean and Tea Leaf

The national coffee shop franchise encourages customers to give to local charities monthly through its Caring Cup campaign. Customers in various regions vote on which charity should receive donations that month, and they are then prompted to buy a ribbon at checkout. The ribbon gives the customer an incentive, a 10 percent discount on drinks for the month. When they purchase the ribbon they can donate any amount of their choice to the chosen charity. Charity partners are local, and range from animal shelters to children's disease research.

Lush North America

Lush, a manufacturer and retailer of organic handmade cosmetics, launched its Charity Pot program in 2007. Charity Pots contain custom-made hand and body lotion products, and 100 percent of the proceeds fund Lush's partner charities around the world. To date, the company has raised more than $4 million for grassroots charities. Lush displays the charity partners prominently at checkout and provides transparency around where the donations go.

Overstock

Overstock created its specialty online market Worldstock to support hundreds of thousands of artisans in the most destitute areas of the world. In doing this, the online retailer identified a segment it cared about as a business, and built a business approach to serve that segment. Some 60 to 70 percent of sales from Worldstock merchandise go directly to the artisans; net profits fund philanthropic projects in developing countries. This specialty market, housed inside a larger marketplace, provides Overstock with an ongoing way to showcase its goodwill, allowing it to making a statement by using its own resources and reach. Worldstock does not drive revenue for the company, but it drives awareness among consumers and aligns closely with Overstock's business affinities.

CVS Caremark

As of October 2014, CVS no longer sells cigarettes or tobacco-based products in more than 7,000 stores. It also partnered with the American Lung Association to help get consumers involved in fundraising for its Lung Force campaign and cause. CVS took a bold stance with consumers in the heavily competitive pharmacy category. It also took the risk of losing a base of customers (smokers) and potential profits, in exchange for loyalty from customers who resonate with the no-cigarette choice. CVS activated engaged customers who were passionate about lung health, and drove new donations for a cause that matches the company's brand values.

TOMS® Shoes

Founded in 2006, TOMS® Shoes promotes the "buy one, give one" concept. For every pair of shoes a customer buys, the company donates a pair to someone in need. The company engages consumers in its "doing good" philosophy by gathering funds through every purchase made and by using those funds to manufacture shoes for people in need. The company's "good" is embedded in its DNA and day-to-day operations, its commitment is long-term, and its model is financially sustainable. TOMS® has proven that sustainability is a social enterprise with the acquisition by Bain Capital in 2014 for a reported $625 million value.

Projects like these employ one or more of four basic principles to engender emotional loyalty between a company and its customers. In fact, the CVS Caremark campaign incorporates all four:

Local

The more personally brands can to connect with consumers based on what *they* care about—not just about what the brand/company cares about—the closer the connection. This phenomenon is often more pertinent to local initiatives and community focus rather than global issues.

Transparent

In a world of short attention spans, brands should not try to overcomplicate effort or impact. Over-marketing and promotion may deliver the wrong message and create concerns about self-promotion. At the same time, apply the KISS ("keep it simple") principle to impact stats—less information often leaves less to scrutinize.

Embedded

If brand efforts aren't connected to the bottom line, reconsider. Customers favor companies that put their own money, products or services where their mouths are, and they enjoy seeing businesses risk themselves as they "do good." It shows skin in the game and builds respect (and cannot be turned off; that's how embedded it is).

Long-lasting

Showing a commitment to a specific cause or initiative over a long period will provide brands with the customer loyalty and reach they seek. Short-term campaigns, while targeted, can often miss many potential customers.

Making better use of crowdfunding

The companies we've discussed have implemented basic crowdfunding campaigns to drive emotional loyalty by raising dollars for causes together with engaged consumers. However, the issue of transparency—as highlighted above—is proving to be more and more important. It takes a great deal of expense and time to set up, manage, and execute this type of campaign, not to mention the subsequent costs to report on the results and drive awareness—either in the short or longer term. As consumers become increasingly sensitive to where their donated dollars are going, they are starting to care more about the amount that brands are spending on their CSR work.

Consumers are also becoming more suspicious about the motive behind a campaign. How much is it about the good cause, and how much about building brand loyalty? This is especially true for the type of fully branded "roll your own" campaigns that companies have traditionally employed. For companies such campaigns are attractive because they allow them to keep a tighter grip on their brands and image. For consumers, they can seem suspiciously opaque.

This is a major shift in consumer thinking and it has led some companies to adopt a new approach by entering into partnership with a crowdfunding platform. Partnerships of this type have an air of openness and built-in checks and balances. They appear less forced and more cooperative than traditional in-house campaigns. They also allow companies to harness much more of the power of socially-enabled crowdfunding as it is practiced by their partner platforms. Campaigns conducted in this way can then become more:

Impression-based
Crowdfunding platforms make full use of the web, embedding a social, viral element to campaigns, which can extend reach and create impressions with new customers, when other campaign options may not be as effective.

Transparent and authentic
The nature of crowdfunding is clear and digestible to consumers. It provides creative options for matching

based on dollars, products, and services, and many crowdfunding campaigns provide ways to target local markets and affinity groups. Done effectively, crowdfunding can more clearly show where the giving is going.

Cost-effective

Rather than the traditional mindset (and high costs) of "roll-your-own" CSR campaigns, crowdfund-focused platform partnerships offer a highly accessible campaign engine that provides the opportunity for lower cost and potentially higher impact programs.

Repeatable

Crowdfunding platforms provide opportunities for long-term engagement based on the fact that they are "always on" and they're designed with the structure, definition, and framework for re-usability.

By taking advantage of this partnership approach, companies can focus on delivering brand products or services, while lending their brand power to help their chosen platforms do what they do best—engage consumers in the digital world. Partnership also demonstrates to consumers that brands are less concerned with brand image and more concerned about creating collaborative, community impact—which, in turn, builds trust.

Given the variety of platforms that have emerged—from financial micro-lending platforms like Kiva to such local cause-related and specialized groups as classroom-focused DonorsChoose—the world of potential crowdfunding partners is far and wide. Some involve corporate partnership opportunities and some require more creative partnership discussions. Some provide more localized options, some cater to loyalty programs, and others enable international support across a wide variety of causes. The choice depends on a brand's CSR goals. There are many to choose from, but a few platforms stand out for reputation and proven results in an evolving space. The first two are cause crowdfunding platforms; the rest offer a combination of peer-to-peer and cause crowdfunding.

GlobalGiving

A charity fundraising website that enables social entrepreneurs and non-profits around the world to raise funds for their causes. They've worked with corporate partners like Dell and Living Social and develop customized Cause Marketing solutions as needed.

DonorsChoose

Enables grade-school teachers in public schools around the country to build crowdfunding campaigns to raise funds for items they need in their classrooms. They've enabled matching programs, promo codes, and other custom solutions for retailers like Crew and Starbucks.

FlipGive

A peer-to-peer fundraising platform designed to

empower school sports programs to fundraise, using the power of consumer brands. Retailers such as Lowe's and Costco have integrated FlipGive into their loyalty programs with consumers, enabling more sales and powering fundraisers in their communities.

CrowdRise

Enables individuals to build fundraisers around their passions, from international aid to pledging their birthdays. They've also driven big dollars for charity by integrating celebrity fundraisers and brand-sponsored fundraisers online, while leveraging online audiences.

Razoo

Offers both peer-to-peer and charity fundraising. Its Giving Day initiatives have driven more than $120 million in donations, and are fueled by a collaborative effort between non-profits and local and national partners.

121Giving

Enables charities to crowdfund dollars from donors to tangibly fund product purchases to meet their operational and organizational needs, including items needed for fundraising or disaster relief efforts. Its eCommerce platform harnesses the collective buying power of hundreds of thousands of U.S. charities, in which brands and retailers can match their needs with exclusive offers and consistent discounts, while consumers can support specific nonprofit needs through crowdfunding capabilities.

The platform also shows where brands' giving is going; brands can measure their social impact while consumers know exactly what their donations are supporting.

While crowdfunding may not be "the golden fleece" for CSR initiatives, it inherently lends itself to many new opportunities that do not currently exist within the traditional CSR model. As it stands today, many crowdfunding practices are very compelling for companies. With consumers spending increasing amounts of time engaged in online activities, including giving, companies have every reason to explore ways of leveraging the crowdfunding channel to build greater emotional loyalty with consumers.

The online giving market continues to grow as consumers become more trusting of the web for philanthropy. According to Achieve's Millennial Impact Report 2012, this is especially true of the millennial generation, with 70 percent preferring digital methods of giving over any other form. As such, companies should consider the best available options for connecting with this socially conscious and predominantly online customer segment. Regardless of the giving demographic, all consumers are tomorrow's stakeholders and companies should take every measure to evolve their CSR efforts now to create the best possible outcomes for tomorrow—and the long term.

But this isn't just a future consideration—even today's stakeholders are shifting to focus much more on a company's impact. According to a *Wall Street Journal* article in April 2014 titled "Social Causes Come Calling": "Shareholders are driving changes in corporate policies and disclosures unthinkable a decade ago, on issues ranging from protecting rain forests to human rights. So far this year, environmental and social issues have accounted for 56 percent of shareholder proposals, representing a majority for the first time, according to accounting firm Ernst & Young LLP. That is up from about 40 percent in the previous two years."

It's clear that consumers want to see a transparent and consistent commitment from companies they support with their checkbooks, and will favor those that take bottom-line risks in their CSR initiatives. In other words, companies that partner with crowdfunding platforms to meet consumer demand, by operationalizing their good and engaging customers in giving with them to important causes, are being rewarded with both emotional and financial loyalty. The demands of the public have evolved and crowdfunding partnerships can provide the kind of fresh thinking and innovation required today to build strong connections between consumers, causes, and companies.

CROWDFUNDING ECONOMIC DEVELOPMENT

Sam Raymond, The World Bank, Dan Marom,
and Kevin Berg Grell

Crowd engagement, market validation, risk dispersal, momentum building: increasingly it is becoming clear that crowdfunding has something to offer even entities that do not otherwise lack for funding. In the last few years more and more multinational organizations and corporations have started using crowdfunding as a means of achieving these larger objectives. Companies like Coca-Cola and Honda have used it to engage with their customers, while others such as IBM have used it as an internal tool to foster innovation and improve existing product development mechanisms.

But it is not just corporations that can benefit from crowdfunding's broad potential. When the objective is to spur and stimulate economic growth in developing countries, it is the original function of crowdfunding that proves most powerful: that of snowballing innovation and widening access to capital.

However, development institutions such as the World Bank are searching for opportunities to harness crowdfunding in a manner that enables market analysis, drives innovation, and facilitates philanthropy. Because the mandate of development institutions is different from other organizations, the use of crowdfunding will differ as well.

The World Bank engages with crowdfunding mechanisms in two general ways: 1) to *harness crowdfunding directly* as a funding mechanism to achieve their objectives, and 2) to *promote crowdfunding indirectly* via interventions on the supply-side (from providers of funding), demand-side (from entrepreneurs and other project creators), and intermediating infrastructure (crowdfunding platforms and related service providers) in order to create a conducive environment for crowdfunding to flourish.

Development institutions are operating in a fast-paced and data-driven environment that requires speedy use of their financial and technical resources, within a robust framework of environmental and social safeguards. They are also justifiably risk-averse. All of which makes crowdfunding an increasingly enticing phenomenon for achieving their goals.

Validating a development project

More than ever before development institutions are trying to use data to inform the way they work. World Bank President Jim Kim often speaks of the "science of delivery" wherein results on the ground drive the testing and scaling of new ways of working.

Impact evaluations have long been used to understand the effectiveness of an intervention ex post facto but increasingly the hunger is for real-time data collection and analysis to inform decision-making. Integrating crowdfunding, crowdsourcing, and/or technology platforms into development project lifecycles offers a readymade way to collect data on various stakeholders in real time.

Macro data taken from multiple crowdfunding platforms can provide guidance on where development institutions could usefully set up public-private partnerships (PPPs) to provide support. For example, if there is a rise in the number of projects to support women and girls, such as those found on Catapult.org and similar platforms, then development institutions could use this data to adjust existing or future interventions in that sector.

Philanthropic crowdfunding continues to grow, generating approximately $1.5 billion in 2013 for social causes which are often within the purview of development institutions. These efforts often fall within major corporates' CSR plans as well. Development institutions cannot possibly participate in or support all of these funding streams, but they should be knowledgeable about such CSR activities: monitoring their efficacy and popularity could be seen as an alternative way of running pilot programs, with the possibility to help scale up successful projects.

On the investment side, corporate partners and development institutions engaged in PPPs should be keenly aware of the crowdfunding bona fides of projects when sourcing and evaluating prospective investment. Development institutions have networks, concessional spending abilities, and a mandate to build capacity in underserved communities. If private sector players can bring scalable and sustainable solutions, then these institutions have a shared responsibility to work together.

Corporate crowdfunding is still at a nascent stage and the involvement of development institutions even more so.

The initial challenge is for institutions like the World Bank to fully carve out their roles within the emerging crowdfunding ecosystems. There are four potential areas where development institutions might engage with crowdfunding: 1) providing *leverage* expertise, social/political reach, and access to investment partners, 2) providing *initial due diligence and seeding* in order to accelerate and de-risk fundraising, 3) providing *safeguards* for investors and project contributors, and 4) serving as a *matching* mechanism between investors and entrepreneurs in support of the crowdfunding platforms.

Leverage

Co-financing and PPP structures are attractive options for development institutions as a means to improve service provision and financial resources. As such, crowdfunding platforms, especially in the debt space, are an appealing way to funnel investment to underserved financial markets. These platforms are especially enticing for their ability to engage diaspora communities, many of which World Bank research suggests are interested in investing in their home country but prefer not to route investment dollars via government initiatives or public sector partners.

In the case of infrastructure and other similar large-scale capital expenditure projects, development institutions are exploring ways of introducing financial products to effectively engage qualified investors. Development institutions partnering with corporates and local regulators and policy-makers should conduct further analysis of crowdfunding value chains to better understand how they can use financial technology tools.

Initial diligence and seeding

Development institutions—and specifically their private sector investment partners such as the Inter-American Development Bank's Multilateral Investment Fund or World Bank's International Finance Corporation—can conduct primary diligence of projects, which offers assurance to potential crowdfunders. Allocation of investment or lending to those projects, via crowdfunding platforms or directly, "seeds" such projects while also demonstrating development institutions' commitment to the work.

Crowdfunding has some overlap with micro-finance, in the sense that the funding requirements for individual projects are relatively low. Therefore there is a significant risk that the larger set-up costs of the due diligence process could limit the scope and viability of crowdfunding. A major challenge is how best to streamline data-collection and processing to bring down the costs of carrying out due diligence. Given the disruptive expansion of crowdfunding platforms into previously unaddressed markets, development institutions should be open to technological innovations, when possible, to achieve this. The robust safeguards frameworks and investment decision frameworks of these organizations can play a catalytic role for corporate and other investors.

In non-investment campaigns, development institutions can play a role in verifying the usefulness of an offering. For example, entrepreneurs in Africa have leveraged the World Bank's Lighting Africa program, which tests and verifies the quality of commercial off-grid lighting products, to establish trust with crowdfunders and/or pre-purchase customers. Development institutions should partner with corporates to provide this verification mechanism in select sectors and countries in order to promote funding for promising early-stage technologies or projects.

Safeguards

Supply-side actors such as investors, project supporters, and consumers are only likely to take part in crowdfunding activities when they can trust the transactions involved. Development institutions, within the context of a PPP, can act as trustees to ensure that crowdfunding mechanisms are used responsibly and sustainably. Strong environmental and social safeguards are the backbone of development institution operating models.

Matching

Development institutions and corporate partners can use matching schemes, which allocate a financial contribution to campaigns that have met a predetermined funding threshold. In certain countries, such schemes can help to promote peer-to-peer lenders and other alternative providers, thus challenging the hegemony of big banks—when advisable.

The British Government's Business Finance Partnership pioneers an innovative program which provided a total of

£60 million [$94 million] (in two tranches) to the peer-to-peer lending platform Funding Circle to promote lending to small and medium businesses. The program "matched" the final 20 percent of qualified debt campaigns. The program expects to generate a total of £580 million ($913 million).

Promoting crowdfunding

Development institutions have a mandate to develop private sector activity, improve investment opportunities, and promote competitive economies. Developing modern and well-functioning financial services is a vital part of these goals. To create an environment in which crowdfunding can function robustly, development institutions focus on three aims:

- Demand-side interventions to inform entrepreneurs in developing countries about the potential of crowdfunding: this will increase the capacity to gain crowdfunding revenue.

- Infrastructure interventions to make it easier to transmit information and capital between funding counterparts. The main objective here is to ensure transparency and security for contributors as well as entrepreneurs and other project creators.

- Supply-side interventions, to a lesser degree, to ensure that investment partners are aware, enabled, and protected in offering their financial, technical and network resources via the Internet.

Demand-side interventions

The developed crowdfunding ecosystems of North America, Europe and Asia are generating more and more well-defined crowdfunding models. Various crowdfunding platforms, industry publications, universities, and service providers are creating online learning materials to capture these models and associated best practices, and these resources are supplemented by a range of expert consultants and mentors accessible through online crowdfunding communities. Unfortunately for entrepreneurs in emerging markets, these materials tend to be Western-centric with limited applicability for more isolated markets, which have separate challenges.

Development institutions have taken part in crowdfunding training events for entrepreneurs and individuals with limited access to traditional financial services. For example, the World Bank conducted a pilot program to help clean-technology entrepreneurs in Kenya, in partnership with the Kenya Climate Innovation Center. These interventions are ad hoc and non-scalable, however, although knowledge is often captured and shared in a systematic way.

Development institutions and corporate partners should subsidize the production of scalable knowledge resources for emerging markets, such as a Massive Open Online Course (MOOC) for crowdfunding. At the micro level, such a guide would be a stand-alone resource for isolated practitioners who need tailored information. At the macro level, a MOOC could measure demand and analyze the strengths, weaknesses, opportunities, and threats related to crowdfunding within emerging markets, as a precursor to bigger initiatives like training seminars or concessional mentorship programs.

Infrastructure interventions

According to the UK-based research and data provider The Crowdfunding Centre, the number of crowdfunding platforms is growing exponentially, with great variety in sophistication and capacity. Sophisticated and well-run crowdfunding platforms with effective integration into underserved communities can have a transformative effect on those communities—and if poorly operated, can represent a lost opportunity. Development institutions should provide technical assistance and support to localized platforms to ensure their legality, efficacy, and global integration.

One critical element of crowdfunding value chains are the payment systems by which funds are collected, escrowed, transferred, or refunded. For example, an effort by Canonical via Indiegogo to sell Ubuntu in 2013 raised $12,814,216 of a $32,000,000 target from 27,635 people in 1 month. Despite the resounding success, there were multiple problems with PayPal across the diverse group of contributors' countries. Development institutions' private sector partners should consider strategic investment and/or providing advice to payment systems organisations operating in emerging markets.

Perhaps the most natural role for development institutions is that of advising government ministries and regulators—and here too they can help to shape the necessary infrastructure for crowdfunding to work effectively. Development institutions should consider strongly pushing investment climate reforms, which in turn lead to evolving financial technologies. As demonstrated by the United States JOBS Act process, legislation and regulation of the crowdfunding industry is a labor-intensive process, but development banks should provide local regulators and policymakers with the tools to develop and implement progressive regulatory regimes at an appropriate pace.

Supply-side interventions
Development institutions have the potential to bring new supply-side groups, such as diaspora communities, into crowdfunding programs. Such groups have long been approached for their charitable giving potential but World Bank research on the Caribbean diaspora, for example, suggests that expatriates are particularly interested in more private sector-led, commercial engagement with their home country. As such, crowdfunding, especially of debt and equity, presents these communities with new options for giving, buying, lending or investing. Development institutions and corporates should work with crowdfunding platforms and financial organizations to align projects with the corresponding diaspora communities around the world.

Knowledge agenda
Development institutions are intrigued by the evolution of the global crowdfunding market, yet lack the data that could help them apply its uses to further their goals. To fill

that gap, a number of research papers have been commissioned and published by development institutions:

- The Multilateral Investment Fund of the Inter-American Development bank explored the use of crowdfunding mechanisms to foster innovation and economic growth in Mexico.

- The European Capacity Building Initiative tendered a similar study on using crowdfunding to foster climate innovation.

- The World Bank commissioned a research project titled "Crowdfunding's Potential for the Developing World" to understand the anticipated market size and to analyse strategies for public and private sector entities to reach this potential.

- The British Government's Department for International Development commissioned a study providing an overview of the crowdfunding industry to help the department assess the need and value of supporting such initiatives—particularly for climate and environment innovations.

Development institutions should continue to gather data from their interventions in a coordinated manner, and fund research especially on regulatory environments that govern crowdfunding. In the spirit of crowdsourcing, research topics and practitioners should be sourced collaboratively with academic and independent researchers.

Corporates and development institutions for crowdfunding
Using crowdfunding to assess and validate worthwhile ideas, drive efficiency, seed initiatives, and manage resources is a potentially far more effective way to grow local and global economies, as compared with traditional methods, and its costs are in keeping with the budgets of these international organizations. Tapping into the wisdom of the crowd at an early stage of a project can help to bring discipline to operations at an early stage, which should help to ensure that such projects are efficiently managed. Development institutions also need to consider how best to scale up projects more rapidly.

However, it's important to remember that generating excitement about the phenomenon of crowdfunding has proven an easy task; navigating the realities of these transformative technologies—especially in emerging markets—is a more serious challenge altogether, and one that has to be tackled collectively.

More than money

Crowdfunding is not just a means of raising money. In 2012 crowdfunding globally was worth $2.7 billion; in 2013 the market grew to over $5 billion; and according to a report commissioned by the World Bank, that number could reach $93 billion by the year 2025. However, even these numbers pale when viewed in the context of some of the global challenges we face today. Crowdfunding is not a one-stop-shop type of solution, but it can be the first stop on a road that leads to prosperity and growth. It is a powerful tool, its potential for influence extending far beyond the mere figures of dollars raised, and in the right hands it has the power to change the world.

Crowdfunding developed as a grassroots movement. By definition it stimulates growth from the bottom upwards. But that doesn't mean that it has nothing to offer big organizations and corporations. On the contrary, only when crowdfunding is both used and supported by these institutions does it truly reach its full potential.

Though cautious estimates project crowdfunding will exceed $90 billion by 2025, these same estimates easily see that number tripling itself when factoring in the involvement of corporations and institutional investors. In this context, global development crowdfunding initiatives become much more interesting when we consider how far their influence could extend, if and when these types of initiatives are leveraged by corporate and governmental entities.

The following examples, taken from the 2013 study "Review of Crowdfunding for Development Initiatives" by Gajda and Walton, demonstrate how four different models of crowdfunding can be used in different ways to support projects of economic, social or environmental benefit. Each model offers a different incentive for investment. The decision about which to use depends on the nature of the project, the amount of funding being sought, and the crowd from which it is being raised.

Donation-based crowdfunding

Donation-based crowdfunding has been used by NGOs for more than a decade. While traditional fundraising usually focuses on people of means, crowdfunding relies on a viral spreading, generating attention and engagement, often making it easier to raise money through traditional mechanisms.

A good example of the use of donation-based crowdfunding comes from Pollinate Energy—a non-profit social enterprise that aims to provide access to affordable clean energy to improve the livelihoods of poor people living in slums in India.

Pollinate Energy raised $10,500 via the crowdfunding platform Chipin (closed operations on March 7, 2013) to finance the establishment of solar light micro-franchises run by five local Indian entrepreneurs. The entrepreneurs, or "pollinators," also received management training under the scheme. The micro-franchises are located in five different regions around Bangalore and serve 100 communities and over 5,000 individuals.

Reward-based crowdfunding

This model is based on an actual (often material) reward given in exchange for the investment. While the parties generally do not define it as a sale, nevertheless this model has become, in some cases, a method of pre-selling a product in order to fund its development and/or production.

The rewards system is usually based on a scaling menu of perks offered for increasing sums of money, and can range from a simple thank you to an all-inclusive trip and a personal tour of the manufacturing process. When the different tiers of rewards are scaled properly, it is possible to achieve a much higher average contribution than with donation-based crowdfunding.

It is worth noting that reward-based crowdfunding and donation-based crowdfunding often rely on similar tactics to generate contributions, i.e. a compelling story and/or emotional presentation. In addition, many reward-based crowdfunding campaigns offer people an opportunity to contribute a relatively small amount of money in exchange for gratitude or goodwill, but otherwise no material reward.

Kenyan company Ushahidi used a reward-based approach to raise the $150,000 it needed to produce the BRCK—an innovative mobile Internet router and connectivity device that works even without electricity connection. The BRCK works much the way a cell phone does, by intelligently and seamlessly switching between Ethernet, Wi-Fi, and 3G or 4G mobile phone networks. Once a SIM card is inserted and the router is connected to a wired or wireless Ethernet connection, the BRCK will automatically get online. If the AC power fails, as it does frequently in the developing world, BRCK falls back on an eight-hour battery without needing to be told. By the end of Ushahidi's campaign, the company had raised $172,107 by pre-selling the device to about 1,000 contributors.

Lending-based crowdfunding

This model of crowdfunding is based on the project owner borrowing money from many people instead of just one source. While this method is used by entrepreneurs, it can also be used by people seeking a loan for personal reasons and, in this regard, lending-based platforms perform the same function as a bank does.

The incentive for both parties is monetary. By offering a loan at lower interest rates than a bank would, a lender can still get a greater return on his money than the interest rate a bank would offer on a savings account; in essence, cutting out the middleman.

While some platforms act as intermediaries, making repayments to lenders, others function simply as match-makers to facilitate the deal between borrower and lenders. As with all forms of crowdfunding, the idea is to mitigate the risk of default by fracturing the loan into many pieces. With more and more corporate financial institutions taking an interest in this type of crowdfunding, it is by far the largest in scope with a transactions total of several billion dollars last year.

One interesting example comes from Tanzania, where a company called Angaza used the SunFunder platform to raise a total of $15,000. The aim was to facilitate the manufacturing and sales of a thousand "Solar Home Systems" in the Mwanza region of Tanzania. The pay-as-you-go solar technology allows customers to pay for clean energy at their own pace. When a customer makes a top-up payment via a mobile money platform, the solar unit is activated for a proportional amount of energy output. Then, once the full price of the product has been paid off, the unit becomes permanently unlocked and customers get free, clean, and reliable energy for the life of the unit.

Annually, 4,800 people are expected to benefit from the project. The predicted total household savings on energy is $5,000 in year one and $75,000 between years 2 and 5 ($5 per family in year one and $75 per family between years 2 and 5—a 30 percent increase in disposable income). The project is expected to avoid a total 100,000 kg of CO_2 emissions (100 kg per family).

Equity-based crowdfunding

This model is based on a return on investment in the form of equity (shares), much like publicly traded companies. In light of this, it is subject to strict regulations and is only available in countries that have provisions allowing this type of equity trading without going public. This can limit the possibility of funding depending on geographical location.

While the incentive in this case is financial and any deal grants the investor legally enforceable rights, for many investors the attraction is also about personal preference, choosing to invest in companies that share moral values and/or social goals.

In 2012, the Dutch solar energy developer Off-Grid Solutions raised $100,000.00 for its WakaWaka Solar Light technology via Symbid, an equity-based crowdfunding platform. A total of 320 investors from around the world were attracted, each receiving returns in the form of dividends. The initiative has enabled the company to develop, manufacture, and market high-tech low-cost solar powered lamps and chargers worldwide.

Following this success, the company launched a buy one/give one "Let's Light Up Haiti" campaign using the Kickstarter and Oneplanetcrowd crowdfunding platforms. The objective was to raise money to construct an assembly plant in Haiti. The initiative has now raised $700,000 from 7,000 investors internationally. As a result, 10,000 WakaWakas will be distributed in Haiti, providing renewable energy for 50,000 people.

Jumpstarting development

Crowdfunding is not a cure-all solution. It has neither the power nor the presumption to replace traditional finance mechanisms. With most of the world's resources controlled by a small percentage of the population, the power of the crowd alone (no matter how large a crowd) to exert financial influence is limited.

However, our societies and our economies are inherently symbiotic. The wealth and resources of the top percentiles would not mean much without a functioning, productive society. Crowdfunding works in a similarly symbiotic way. While it started as an alternative method of finance, its real potential for growth is in its power to stimulate, supplement, and augment.

Donation-based crowdfunding cannot replace the wealthy philanthropists of the world. The charitable donations made by Bill and Linda Gates easily dwarf any and all crowdfunding projects worldwide. Yet the momentum and engagement created by a successful crowdfunding campaign can motivate people to donate to a cause. One need only look at the recent Ice Bucket Challenge campaign by the ALS Association as an example.

When properly wielded and supplemented by other resources, crowdfunding has the potential to be a real game-changer in terms of local and global development. The funding requirements involved are relatively modest. It does not take a big development bank to exercise these opportunities for economic development; it takes information and advocacy, and that is exactly what these crowdfunding initiatives provide.

5

BRINGING
CORPORATE
CROWDFUNDING
IN-HOUSE

Paul Brody, EY

It is widely assumed that venture capitalists and corporate R&D executives are thoughtful risk takers, carefully placing bets on new but risky technologies and products, seeking a balance of return on investment with a mix of a few big winners and a lot of small losses. Reality is more prosaic: VC investments and corporate R&D spending is remarkably risk-averse, focusing on me-too investments around similar products. Nothing sums this up better than the suggestion I got from one VC on my own start-up plans: "Come back when you're cash flow positive."

While insiders have long known these organizations to be fairly conservative, the full extent of the problem was not visible until the recent rise of crowdfunding websites like Kickstarter and Indiegogo. Consumers, it seems, are the real visionaries and risk takers. From immersive virtual reality (Occulus) to Smartwatches (Pebble) and smart light bulbs (Lifx), start-ups that were passed on by professional "experts" are getting funded by consumers and going on to build substantial businesses.

Enterprises are now looking to bring that same capability into their R&D programs, and in doing so, address their own inability to identify and pursue successful dissipative innovation.

The crisis in corporate R&D

Research and Development in large companies is in crisis. Spending on corporate R&D remains strong and patents, for one, are at record highs. With 6,809 patents, IBM led the league table again in 2013 followed by Samsung (4,675), Canon (3,825), Sony (3,098), Microsoft (2,660), Panasonic (2,601), Toshiba (2,416), HonHai (2,279), Qualcomm (2,013), and LG Electronics (1,947). Patent awards are generally highly correlated with corporate R&D spending, though some companies (IBM in particular) seem able to earn significantly more patents for the same R&D spending than others.

If you look carefully at that list of top patent award winners, you'll notice that something is missing; the companies widely regarded as the world's most innovative. Apple, for example, only comes in at number 13, and Google at 11. And with the exception of Samsung, not a single company in the top ten shows up on any of three recent notable lists of top innovators:

Rank	Forbes	Fast Company	MIT
1	salesforce.com	Google	Illumina
2	Alexion Pharma	Bloomberg Philanthropy	Tesla
3	ARM Holdings	Xiaomi	Google
4	Unilever Indonesia	Dropbox	Samsung
5	Regeneron Pharma	Netflix	salesforce.com
6	Amazon	Airbnb	DropBox
7	BioMarin Pharma	Nike	BMW
8	CP All	ZipDial	Third Rock Ventures
9	VMWare	DonorsChoose.org	Square
10	Aspen Pharmacare	Yelp	Amazon

Indeed, while corporate R&D departments are agreed to excel at incremental process and technology improvement, they are increasingly regarded as unable to deliver real breakthrough innovations that could result in significant changes in a company's position in the market.

Even as corporate R&D organizations have excelled and structured the process of continuous improvement, the importance of breakthrough and disruptive innovation have become much greater. Historically, viable strategies for corporations included managing the installed base and working as a fast-follower to new entrants in the market that came up with significant innovations.

The gradual infusion of software into all forms of product, however, has changed the economics of innovation and, with it, the economics of R&D. Software-based industries have three key differences that make them unusual compared to all other businesses: they offer increasing returns to scale without limit. While almost every manufacturing or service industry has limits on the impact of economies of scale, software unit costs only ever go down.

The result of all of this is winner-take-all economics. And, as the "Internet of things" turns everything into a digitally connected software product, it's spreading out from software into other spaces in the technology industry and from there into other industries. To see how quickly and dramatically this can take place, look at the mobile phone industry. In 2007 half a dozen different companies shared in the profits of the industry. By 2011 just two companies had the entire industry profits:

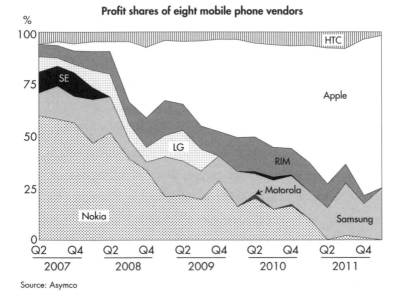

Profit shares of eight mobile phone vendors

Source: Asymco

Winner-take-all economics leaves no place for fast followers. If your careful plans for incremental process improvement are disrupted by a successful new entrant, your odds of recovering are slim. The result has been a huge shift in corporate strategic focus towards innovation, especially those innovations which may re-arrange markets.

Bingeing on start-ups

If corporate R&D represents the perfection of continuous process improvement, then Silicon Valley has come to represent the perfection of the "ready for disruption" business model. Start-ups represent the integration of technology and business model in a single package, all put together without regard to legacy customers and cost considerations and using the latest technology.

A later-stage start-up has product, technology, and a small group of initial customers. The offering has been honed by the market place and usually represents a significantly better value than what industry incumbents are offering. The customers for these start-ups are taking big risks going with an unknown new company that may or may not be around for a while. The reward should be commensurately large.

In short, the start-up is the ideal ready-to-scale package— product, technology, and value proposition just waiting for branding and sales teams to scale it around the world. And that is what has happened. Big technology companies in the U.S. have learned to acquire their innovations, treating Silicon Valley as a market place for outsourced R&D.

On average, IBM and Google each acquire one new company every month. Apple has made over thirty acquisitions in the last ten years and Amazon has made over forty. In every case, the bulk of acquisitions are not large companies with significant brands, but smaller companies with proven products and skills but little established distribution and branding.

Crowdfunding opportunities

Start-ups are attractive because they are market-tested packages of product and business model, but they often lack true insider insights and expertise into a particular market or customer base. The opportunity for corporations to leverage crowdfunding is right there: at the intersection of expert insider knowledge of markets and clients with the ability to market-test innovations.

If enterprises can find a way to leverage crowdfunding in their own development process, the benefits are likely to be enormous. The single most important one, by far, is the ability of crowdfunding to help companies de-risk new product investments. Having a committed customer base for the initial production run is a far more compelling data-set than a market survey.

From a process perspective, crowdfunding can help address one of the key challenges in the product development process: how to objectively manage funding decisions. One of the biggest drains on innovation budgets is the loss of products that die far too late in the development process. Crowdfunding provides an early market test that could result in a quicker cut-off for unsuccessful products and strategies.

Finally, crowdfunding initiatives are the most compelling way to build community and insight around future products. The pages of Kickstarter projects are often filled with thousands of suggestions and messages from customers who have pledged their commitment to the product concept. This level of engagement is far higher than what most companies achieve in the product development stage. It's also critical to their success; research by IBM has shown that most companies have found that it is their customers who provide the most valuable innovation ideas in the long run.

Crowdfunded obstacles (real and imagined)

Despite the many attractions of crowdfunding, it is not without risk and complexity. Most notably, nearly all crowdfunding projects that involve any kind of manufacturing run shockingly far behind schedule. It's not uncommon for the benefits of a Kickstarter project, for example, to show up as much as a year later than planned. Few crowdfunding projects are built with realistic timelines. Not a problem for start-ups, perhaps, but a big issue for companies with brand names and vocal customers. Enterprises that want to leverage crowdfunding need to make sure that they properly plan out and vet their product development and manufacturing processes to manage expectations from clients. This also represents an opportunity for established companies with strong manufacturing, supply chain, and quality organizations that can do a better job delivering on product commitments than typical start-up operations.

The other big obstacle cited by companies is secrecy. Product development processes today are shrouded in secrecy, along with product roadmaps and timelines. This is the only really bad reason to avoid using crowdfunding. While surprises are delightful (at least the good kind), they are also over-rated. Take the lesson of another big trend: open innovation. More and more companies have found that copying an innovation is much harder than it looks and customers are not often fooled. Consequently while the risk of being copied is modest, the risk of investing heavily in a failure is much, much larger. The result is that, on balance, the price paid in secrecy is more than repaid in reduced risk.

Sony has made successful use of a "split the difference"

approach to secrecy. When it set up corporate crowdfunding campaigns for its new e-paper watch (see page 103) and Qrio electronic door lock in Japan, the product was shown without any Sony branding. This allowed the company to test the concept with consumers without relying on the momentum provided by a brand or tipping their hand to potential competitors.

Of course, crowdfunding doesn't work for everything. It's not necessary for run-of-the-mill improvements to processes and products; corporate R&D departments have largely mastered that. Where it will work best is for new product concepts targeted at an existing customer base, with one important caveat: crowdfunding inside the enterprise will be difficult when the value proposition is highly disruptive to the current business model.

The future of corporate innovation spending

Like any successful investment approach, enterprises need to manage a portfolio of options when it comes to innovation. Over the last two decades, the portfolio has grown from internal R&D projects to include external acquisitions as a routine activity. The challenge for corporate leaders will be to place crowdfunding into the context of all their other options and to fund and manage it accordingly. I believe there are two key dimensions that innovation investors in the enterprise need to balance: time (sooner vs. later) and form (incremental vs. disruptive). In that context, corporate crowdfunding fits best around near-term but potentially disruptive innovations.

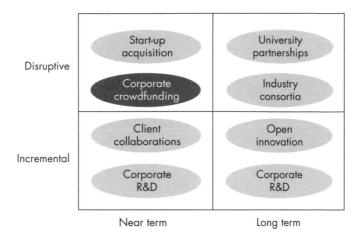

Though likely to be less radical than separate start-ups, crowdfunding will allow insiders in the enterprise to quickly market test ideas that fall outside proven product categories and value propositions.

Despite some significant challenges, crowdfunding is perhaps the single biggest opportunity for transformation in corporate R&D in decades. After many efforts to replicate the discipline of the market within the enterprise, this is the only one that will truly bring that discipline directly in-house. The result will be more innovation taken with less capital put at risk—a huge incentive for in-house researchers to polish their business skills. A new era of corporate R&D awaits.

CONCLUSION

Kevin Berg Grell, Dan Marom, and Richard Swart

The era of corporate crowdfunding

There are those who say that all knowledge is finite and has existed since the dawn of time; that our greatest inventions are in fact discoveries, "remembered" or deduced by smart individuals; and that it is therefore impossible to truly create something new. Whether or not that is true is a matter best left to philosophers and theologians, but what we do know is that every good idea or worthwhile invention takes on a life of its own.

The greatest inventions have been quickly adopted and adapted by the masses, entrenched in every aspect of our lives. The Internet, for example, was developed by researchers for the US Department of Defense's Advanced Research Project Agency, but has since evolved to connect billions of people around the world. Crowdfunding may have started out as an alternative source of funding for creative projects and start-ups, but it will not remain so. We have already seen it used by some of the world's biggest companies and best known brands to enhance every aspect of their business, from research and development down to philanthropic activities.

As a marketing tool, we've seen how crowdfunding can expand a client base and create new markets, while also redefining the standard for an engaged and loyal customer. As a force for innovation, we've seen how crowdfunding can combine a thousand voices and a million thoughts into one great idea that can change the world. And as a support mechanism for corporate social responsibility, we've seen how it can reinforce the connection between a corporation and the public by making them partners in support of good causes.

Whether it's stronger marketing, faster innovation, or a better image, and whether it involves using a public platform or an internal campaign, the common thread is the connection that crowdfunding provides between the company and the crowd. Customers and clients are no longer passive recipients waiting to be served. They can be more than simply judges who choose between the different options based on the end product. They can be partners, a part of the process from conception to marketing.

This engagement has been shown to matter. The 2014 Rosetta Consulting Engagement Study suggests that companies with an engaged customer base outperform their competitors, being up to 2.2 times more likely to experience an increase in market share. Likewise in their book *Leading on the Edge of Chaos*, authors Emmet C. Murphy and Mark A. Murphy state that gaining a 2 percent customer retention has the same effect as decreasing costs by 10 percent, while Gallup's daily tracking of the U.S. economy suggests that 23 percent of increases in terms of share of wallet, profitability, revenue, and relationship growth stem from increased customer engagement.

But while these numbers would be impressive on a quarterly or annual performance report, the benefits are not limited to the business sector. Many organizations, institutions, and even governments have used crowdfunding tools to leverage their assets and increase their influence. And as they do so, crowdfunding mechanisms become integrated into more systems in our economy and other aspects of our lives.

Therein lies the real potential of crowdfunding. It has the power to synergize with other mechanisms and leverage them to greater effect. As our experience and understanding of crowdfunding develop, we will find new methods and ways of using it to our advantage.

Where next?

Some of these new developments may be hard to foresee; others are simply logical evolutions of processes that have already begun. The day is not far off when all banks will have their own peer-to-peer lending platforms, or where we use crowdfunding to determine which TV shows get made and which direction they will follow; where students can apply for a scholarship or financial aid from their peers; or when a portion of a city's or country's spending is directed by the wisdom of the crowd.

What began as a novelty and then developed into what some would call a fashionable trend now continues to grow at a formidable rate. Crowdfunding has increased more than ten times in scope over the past four years and with an annual growth rate estimated at 167 percent, a global funding volume of $34.4 billion is projected for 2015. But though it may change the way we interact, consume, and develop, crowdfunding's future doesn't look all that different from its present. We are not headed towards the downfall of all banks and investment firms. Crowdfunding will not abolish the need for institutional money, or R&D labs, or marketing firms.

The future of crowdfunding is integration. We hardly ever notice when we are in the midst of a new evolution. The world seems to change so gradually about us, and it isn't until much later that we look back and realize the magnitude of the change that we have undergone and its importance in our lives. When crowdfunding evolves from alternative to mainstream, from novelty to mundane, that is when we will be able to look back and say it changed the world.

The Internet, for example, is perhaps the greatest invention of the last century, and it is definitely the one that has had the greatest impact on this one (so far). But when comparing our lives before the World Wide Web and after, there are fundamental similarities. We still wake up every morning and go to work or to school. We watch TV shows and read the newspaper. We read, we play, we meet up and gossip. And while every one of these activities may be done differently now, in essentials they have not changed. As Paul Simon eloquently put it, "after changes we are more or less the same."

That is not to say the world isn't changing. That change may be subtle, it may be gradual, but it is persistent. We call it globalization, but it is far more pervasive a phenomenon. We are growing closer to each other, more interdependent, and with every new major technological or social achievement this effect increases. The phenomenon of collaborative consumption, of which crowdfunding is a component, is just one of the many forces that have been driving us in the same direction for hundreds of years.

As a species we keep trying, both consciously and subconsciously, to find new ways and better tools to connect us, and that is what crowdfunding does. It connects people. It brings people together over common interests, common goals, and common beliefs. And the more people who are connected, the greater its reach becomes. The greater crowdfunding's reach is, the more people it connects. One of the reasons crowdfunding is growing at such a fast pace is that it is a phenomenon that feeds itself. It enhances other systems, but also itself. The more people who are connected, the closer our global community becomes, the more powerful crowdfunding becomes. So what does the future hold for the three main aspects of crowdfunding that we have discussed: marketing, innovation, and corporate social responsibility?

Crowdsourced advertising campaigns such as the ALS Ice Bucket Challenge show us how marketing can be completely driven by social sharing and social dynamics. Not unlike crowdfunding campaigns gone viral, this mechanism can prove an extremely efficient way to get a specific message across to a huge audience. We believe that corporations will see such crowdsourced advertising as an opportunity to push information about their CSR agendas as well as their product development, even when this means giving up control of the messaging. Given that such campaigns build upon the same social mechanisms as crowdfunding, we believe that corporations have an opportunity to couple the two models—crowdsourced advertising and crowdfunding—in a similar way to successful "activism" platforms such as Avaaz and 38 Degrees.

In the field of innovation, we have seen how corporations use crowdfunding as a tool for market testing; where once there were focus groups and customer surveys, today there are thousands of people ready to give their feedback and support via social media driven campaigns including crowdfunding campaigns. Not only do corporations reach larger groups of potential customers, they get much more reliable signals of market interest, because the crowds are to some extent voting with their wallets. For these reasons, we believe that crowdfunding will disrupt the entire scope of innovation within large corporations, enabling more products to be tested, and elevating the R&D decision process because the company is less exposed to the inaccuracies of traditional market research.

We have also seen how companies like IBM use employees in crowdfunding campaigns to boost innovation and make internal improvements. And we have seen how companies can use crowdfunding as a tool to direct their investments and acquisitions, lowering their overall risk. By combining these two initiatives, a corporation can leverage the expertise of its own employees to guide investment decisions. This looks like low-hanging fruit for any corporation with significant in-house expertise, and thus an investment model that we expect will see the light of day as an extension of current employee investment programs.

Crowdsourcing ideation platforms are well known already. Dell's Ideastorm and GE's partnership with quirky. com are just two examples. We believe that in the near future, these models will be paired with both reward-based and investment-based crowdfunding. The corporation's role will expand from the sole investor role of today, to a lead-investor or fund-matcher tomorrow. The corporation's incentive is unchanged: source information about public interest and use this information to support or acquire the companies that resonate with the crowd.

Crowdfunding's benefits for the CSR process are already well documented, and we believe that the biggest change here will be deeper integration of crowdfunding into existing programs. We expect that the major disruptions will be for civic crowdfunding (i.e. communities proposing target projects for corporations to support), customer-directed charity, and internal crowdfunding for CSR (this model will include elements of fund-matching as well).

The big disruption for CSR programs will be one of reverse-influence. Corporations will to a lesser degree cherry-pick projects to support, but they will rely heavily on crowdfunding as the selection mechanism. This presents a set of new challenges because to some extent corporations will lose control over the selection mechanism and over the scope of their CSR efforts. While crowd mechanisms can be extremely efficient in terms of advocacy and information sourcing, the people behind these developments are not necessarily in line with corporate strategy. Exactly how corporations will handle this challenge is subject to much research interest, and yet another reason to follow the progress of crowdfunded CSR very closely in the near future.

A new era

Crowdfunding is primarily a form of finance and as such it continues to grow, as indicated by the towering figures of transactions in the industry. However, its power lies in the fact that it provides many other benefits; that it is about more than just money. This quality in particular is what synergizes so well with recent social and economic developments. In a globalized world it is not enough to be good at one thing. Investors and venture capitalists who offer only money are shortchanging their partners, and companies who see their customers as mere consumers are not only shortchanging them, they're missing opportunities.

Crowdfunding is about combining resources into something that is greater than the sum of its parts. It's about everybody getting back more than they put in. And it's about creating symbiotic relationships. Investors and customers are more than just sources of money, they can become real partners, and that kind of relationship makes both sides stronger.

We have seen how crowdfunding can help companies and organizations improve their image, their reach, and even their capacity for innovation, but what effect are corporations having on the world of crowdfunding in return? When a company like GE partners with an online crowdfunding platform, providing resources, experience, and expertise to crowdfunding entrepreneurs, it doesn't just benefit those entrepreneurs, it benefits the entire field.

Crowdfunding will become a critical strategy for corporations in the future. And the future of corporate innovation and customer engagement will be integrated with the growth of crowdfunding. The future seems to be headed to a massive realignment between corporations and their customers and partners—and crowdfunding will drive much of this change.

As a relatively new invention, crowdfunding will change and evolve over time. As companies catch on to its advantages, crowdfunding will become more widespread and the benefits it brings to its corporate users will increase accordingly. This mutualism represents a chance for crowdfunding to evolve into something new—an opportunity to grow beyond the world of entrepreneurial finance. Its relatively unexplored terrain will be shaped by those who take the field, and while it represents many benefits for forward-thinking organizations, it represents an even greater opportunity to us, the wider public. We have seen some examples of how effective a tool crowdfunding can be when wielded properly, but we have barely begun to scratch the surface. Crowdfunding may have started out as the champion of innovators and entrepreneurs, but it belongs to everyone and it is still in its infancy. Where we go from here is up to us.

BIOGRAPHIES

Co-founder and CEO of APEN Designs, which is a collaborative platform for start-ups and SMEs, **Dr Kevin Berg Grell** oversees product/market development along with content creation, as it pertains to business economics issues. Besides this venture, he consults for private companies, development banks, etc. on the implications of online retail investing, including crowdfunding.

Kevin earned his doctorate in Business Administration in 2011 with the defense of his dissertation, "On Venture Capital," which was subsequently published in book form and an individual chapter called "Venture Capital Budgeting" was also published in *Journal of Corporate Finance*. Before this, he earned an MSc in mathematics and economics with a thesis on "Credit Risk and Asymmetric Information." His professional interests include emerging financial models, start-up management, and economic design.

Previously, Kevin was the research director for Crowdsourcing.org and the lead author of *The 2013 Crowdfunding Industry Report* published by Massolution.

Dr Dan Marom is a renowned expert in the field of crowdfunding and the author of the pioneering book *The Crowdfunding Revolution*. Dan advises international organizations such as the World Bank, the European Commission, and other corporates and ventures operating in the crowdfunding field. More about Dan can be found at www.danmarom.com.

Dr Richard Swart has emerged as the global expert in developments in crowdfunding. A founding board member of the Crowdfunding Professional Association (CfPA) and the Crowdfunding Intermediary Regulatory Advocates (CFIRA), he has more than twenty years' experience in the entrepreneurial ecosystem, and uses his extensive global network to help educate and mentor firms, policy holders, and businesses. He is a highly trusted expert resource for governments, academics and crowdfunding platforms.

He has lectured on crowdfunding developments in Europe, the UK, Africa, the Middle East, and throughout the United States, and is a board member and strategic advisor to firms in the crowdfunding and alternative investing space. He was recently appointed Crowdfunding and Alternative Research Scholar in the Haas School of Business, UC Berkeley.

Richard was the lead author on the World Bank's 2013 report, "Crowdfunding's Potential for the Developing World." In the same year he partnered with the University of Cambridge to complete the first country-level study of alternative finance: "The Rise of Future Finance: The UK Alternative Finance Benchmarking Report." With Crowdfund Capital Advisors he authored "How Does Crowdfunding Impact Job Creation, Revenue and Professional Investor Interest?"

Richard is co-founder of Exovate.co, a boutique advisory firm serving corporations and foundations with crowd-based business models and strategy.

Ana Coelho Brandes started her academic career in 2009 with her Bachelor of Science in Economic Sciences at the Technische Universität Dresden, Germany, with a specialization in Marketing and Management. During her ERASMUS year at the Universidade Nova de Lisboa she put a stronger emphasis on quantitative techniques and risk management. In 2013 she started her MSc in International Business at Aston University, Birmingham and wrote her dissertation on "New Venture Capital Trends – Corporate Venture Capital and Crowdfunding."

Paul Brody is a partner at EY, focused on digital transformation and growth in the technology sector. Prior to joining EY, Paul was the global industry leader for electronics at IBM and a founding member of IBM's Industry Academy. He also spent time at a number of start-ups including the first mobile network operator in West Africa. Paul started his career at McKinsey & Co. in Los Angeles.

Paul has more than twenty years of experience developing digital strategies for technology companies, managing transitions from fixed to mobile computing and is now focused on the Internet of things and the rise of distributed economic and computing infrastructures like BitCoin.

Paul has a degree in Economics from Princeton University and a Certificate in African Studies, also from Princeton. He has authored numerous publications throughout his career on the topics of digital transformation in everything from consumer marketing to supply chain management.

Mark Courtney is the co-founder of Austin-based 121Giving, an online platform that aims to revolutionize charitable fundraising, corporate social responsibility (CSR) programs and crowdfunding initiatives by harnessing the buying power and product needs of hundreds of thousands of U.S. charities. A social innovator and self-described servant leader, Mark combines his extensive enterprise solutions background with a collaborative vision focused on a better, more connected world for all. Before launching 121Giving, Mark was involved in large-scale technology and change-management initiatives at leading consulting and start-up firms.

Liz Deering is co-founder of 121Giving. She is a social entrepreneur and risk-taker, whose career love for start-ups took root early on when she joined Boston-based Picasa while earning a Master's Degree in graphic design. She then spent more than fifteen years in marketing, interactive technologies and account management positions at both category-disrupting start-ups and traditional nonprofit organizations—experiences that fueled her passion to launch 121Giving.

Anna Grosman is an Assistant Professor in Strategy at Aston University, Birmingham, UK, since 2013. Her past research examines corporate governance of established and young firms, and in particular, how institutional environments, ownership networks, board structures, firm transparency, executive compensation and social capital influence a firm's strategic decisions and outcomes. Anna holds a PhD from Imperial College London. She gained extensive industry experience as she worked for Koch Industries as a Director of Strategy, Corporate Development and Mergers and Acquisitions for four years. Prior to that, she worked for over six years in investment banking and corporate finance for CIBC World Markets, Citigroup and Close Brothers.

Josef Holm co-founded and is the CEO of Tubestart.com, the first-of-its-kind crowdfunding platform for video creators and filmmakers. In 2014 he also founded Krowdster.co, the first crowdfunding campaign analytics, optimization and promotion SaaS application based on big data, machine learning and predictive analytics.

Josef has seventeen years of start-up, business development, digital marketing, social web and affiliate marketing experience. He sits on the PR subcommittee of the Crowdfunding Professional Association (CFPA). He has also been a featured speaker at several crowdfunding conferences, including Kickercon, and is regularly featured in a number of publications such as *CrowdFundBeat*, *USA Today*, *Wired*, *LA Business Journal* and *Fast Company*.

Mentored by Richard Swart, **Robert Lusk** spent time at UC Berkeley in its Program for Innovation in Entrepreneurial and Social Finance, researching the future of crowdfunding and the economic implications. He has had the opportunity to visit Capitol Hill to discuss the state of the JOBS Act and current regulation and has worked on multiple research projects and papers. A natural entrepreneur, he is working with several companies across various industries to integrate crowdfunding mechanisms that will improve the ways they raise capital and connect with their consumers.

Zack Miller has been growing investment businesses for the past decade. He is General Partner, Head of Investor Community at OurCrowd. Previously, Zack held senior leadership positions and consulted to some of the top next-generation finance sites including OurCrowd, Seeking Alpha, Lending Club, Wall Street Survivor, Covestor, and SigFig. Zack began his career in finance as an equities analyst at a multinational hedge fund. He is also the author of *Tradestream your Way to Profits: Building a Killer Portfolio in the Age of Social Media* (Wiley, 2010) and runs the popular investing website Tradestreaming.com. Zack received his MBA from Northwestern's Kellogg School of Management and his BA in Economics from Harvard.

Stephen Paljieg is a Senior Director of Growth and Innovation with the Kimberly-Clark Corporation. He is a serial innovator in the consumer goods industry, both in the U.S. and abroad. Between 2005 and 2007, his track record of success included an unprecedented run of 5 IRI Top 10 Non-Food Pacesetter Products, including Tide with a Touch of Downy, Tide Coldwater, and Febreze Noticeables.

Most recently Stephen's passions have turned to the use of open innovation networks to externally source innovation and, most importantly, alter the relationship between a brand and its users. Since 2010, the Huggies MomInspired™ program he pioneered has been instrumental in defining Huggies® as a "curator of innovation" versus simply a manufacturer of diapers and wipes.

Stephen's efforts to create open innovation networks have been recognized with 2010 SPIKE (Social Product Innovation) Awards in both Consumer Packaged Goods and People's Choice categories.

Sam Raymond is a Consultant with infoDev's Access to Finance Program. His work with the World Bank Group centers on the development of projects that address the challenges faced by entrepreneurs in acquiring financing to scale businesses and create jobs. These projects include market-access programs, angel investor promotion initiatives, online technology portals to promote diaspora investment, investment models for business accelerators, and, most recently, analytical work on crowdfunding. Prior to joining the World Bank Group, Sam worked as Research and Staff Assistant to Speaker of the United States House of Representatives Nancy Pelosi.

Erit Yellen has spent over fifteen years in the sports industry as an executive working mostly for and representing professional athletes, organizations and initiatives in public relations, fundraising and cause marketing. Erit founded EYA Sports PR in 2004, a first-of-its-kind public relations firm for individuals. EYA was acquired by PMK/HBH in 2007 where Erit served as the company's first Director of Sports. She then left to continue her advocacy and consulting work. A former D1 College Athlete at the University of Wisconsin, Erit has been a guest lecturer in Sports PR and Social Change at USC's Annenberg Institute of Sports, Media & Society.

BIBLIOGRAPHY

Compiled by Anna Grosman and Ana Brandes

Agrawal, A., Catalini, C., and Goldfarb, A. (2011). "The Geography of Crowdfunding," *NBER Working Paper*, No. w16820. Available from SSRN: http://ssrn.com/abstract=1770375 [accessed June 5, 2014].

Ahuja, G. (2000). "Collaboration Networks, Structural Holes and Innovation: A Longitudinal Study," *Administrative Science Quarterly*, 45, 425–455.

Baldwin, C. and Von Hippel, E. (2011). "Modeling a Paradigm Shift: From Producer Innovation to User and Open Collaborative Innovation," *Organization Science*, 22(6), 1399–1417.

Belleflamme, P., Lambert, T., and Schwienbacher, A. (2011). "Crowd-funding: Tapping the Right Crowd," *CORE Discussion Paper*, 32.

Bernstein, P. (2014). "American Express Partners with Seed&Spark to Distribute Film," *Indiewire* [online]. Available from: http://www.indiewire.com/article/american-express-partners-with-seed-spark-to-distribute-films [accessed January 15, 2014].

Birkinshaw, J. and Duke, L. (2013). "Employee-Led Innovation," *Business Strategy Review* [online], 2, 46–51. Available from: http://www.london.edu/bsr [accessed November 19, 2014].

Blomqvist, K. and Levy, J. (2006). "Collaboration Capability—A Focal Concept in Knowledge Creation and Collaborative Innovation in Networks," *International Journal of Management Concepts and Philosophy*, 2(1), 31–48.

Burt, R. S. (2004). "Structural Holes and Good Ideas," *American Journal of Sociology*, 110(2), 349–399.

Bynghall, S. (2014). "Is Internal Crowdfunding in the Enterprise Set to Take Off?" *Getting Results From Crowds* [online]. Available from: http://www.resultsfromcrowds.com/insights/is-internal-crowdfunding-in-the-enterprise-set-to-take-off/ [accessed July 2, 2014].

Chandler, A. D. (1990). *Scale and Scope*. Cambridge, MA: Belknap.

Chesbrough, H. (2003). *Open Innovation: The New Imperative for Creating and Profiting from Technology.* Boston, MA: Harvard Business School Publishing.

Chesbrough, H. (2006). "Open Innovation: A New Paradigm for Understanding Industrial Innovation." In: Chesbrough, H., Vanhaverbeke, W., and West, J. (eds.). *Open Innovation: Researching a New Paradigm.* Oxford University Press.

Christensen, C. M. (1997). *The Innovator's Dilemma: When New Technologies Cause Great Firms to Fail.* Boston, MA: Harvard Business School Press, 1997.

Collins, L. and Pierrakis, Y. (2012). *The Venture Crowd: Crowdfunding Equity Investment Into Business.* Nesta.

DiMicco, J., Millen, D. R., Geyer, W., Dugan, C., Brownholtz, B., and Muller, M. (2008). "Motivations for Social Networking at Work," *CSCW Proceedings of the 2008 ACM Conference on Computer Supported Cooperative Work*, 711–720.

Elis, N. (2013). "GE Becomes First Corporate Partner for Equity Crowdfunding in OurCrowd Deal," *JPost* [online]. Available from: http://www.jpost.com/Business/Business-News/GE-becomes-first-corporate-partner-for-equity-crowdfunding-in-OurCrowd-deal-330592 [accessed June 10, 2014].

Feldmann, N., Gimpel, H., Muller, M., and Geyer, W. (2014). "Idea Assessment Via Enterprise Crowdfunding: An Empirical Analysis of Decision-Making Styles," *Twenty Second European Conference on Information Systems.*

Fisher, A. (2013). "How IBM Bypasses Bureaucratic Purgatory," *Fortune* [online]. Available from: http://fortune.com/2013/12/04/how-ibm-bypasses-bureaucratic-purgatory/ [accessed August 30, 2014].

Helander, M., Lawrence, R., and Li, Y. (2007). "Looking for Great Ideas: Analyzing the Innovation Jam," *2007 KDD Proceedings.*

Hui, J. S., Greenberg, M. D., and Gerber, E. M. (2014). "Understanding the Role of Community in Crowdfunding Work," *Proceedings of the 17th ACM Conference on Computer Supported Cooperative Work & Social Computing*, 62–74.

IBM (2014). Our People – IBM Research. PhD Michael Muller. http://researcher.watson.ibm.com/researcher/view.php?person=us-michael_muller [accessed October 23, 2014].

Lang, L. (2014). "VC Invests in LOVESPACE Via Crowdcube,"
Crowdcube blog [online]. Available from: http://www.crowdcube.com/
blog/2014/06/06/dn-capital-invests-alongside-crowd-lovespace/
[accessed June 7, 2014].

LeGoues, F. (2014). Interviewed by Grosman, A., November 24, 2014.

Leiponen, A. and Helfat, C. E. (2010). "Innovation objectives,
knowledge sources, and the benefits of breadth," *Strategic
Management Journal*, 31, 224–236.

Luckerson, V. (2014). "This New Kind of Kickstarter Could
Change Everything. IBM is Giving Money to Its Employees for
Crowdfunded Projects," *TIME* [online]. http://business.time.
com/2014/01/20/ibm-internal-enterprise-crowdfunding-mimics-
kickstarter/ [accessed July 2, 2014].

Mathers, B. (2014). Interviewed by Brandes, A. and Grosman, A.,
November 26, 2014.

Millen, D.R. and Fontaine, M.A. (2003). "Multi-team Facilitation of
Very Large-Scale Distributed Meetings." *2003 ECSCW Proceedings*.

Muller, M., Geyer, W., Soule, T., Daniels, S., and Cheng, Li-Te
(2013). "Crowdfunding Inside the Enterprise: Employee-Initiatives
for Innovation and Collaboration," *Session: Crowdwork and Online
Communities*.

Muller, M. (2014a). Interviewed by Brandes, A. and Grosman, A.,
August 27, 2014.

Muller, M., Geyer, W., Soule, T., and Wafer, J. (2014). "Geographical
and Organizational Commonalities in Enterprise Crowdfunding,"
CSCW 2014 Technology and Information Workers.

Nielsen, J. (2006). "Participation Inequality: Encouraging More
Users to Contribute." Available from: http://www.nngroup.com/
articles/participation-inequality/ [accessed November 9, 2014].

Rogers, E. M. (2003). *Diffusion of Innovations* (5th ed.). New York:
Free Press.

Root, A. (2013). "IBM's Internal Crowdfunding Rewards Employee
Innovation." Available from: http://www.crowdsourcing.org/
editorial/ibms-internal-crowdfunding-rewards-employee-
innovation/28457 [accessed July 2, 2014].

Sahin, I. (2006). "Detailed Review of Rogers' Diffusion of Innovations
Theory and Educational Technology-Related Studies Based on

Rogers' Theory," *The Turkish Online Journal of Educational Technology*, 5 (2). Available from ISSN: 1303-6521.

School for Social Entrepreneurs (SSE) Australia (2014). "ING DIRECT Offers a $100,000 Crowdfunding Initiative," *SSE Australia*. Available from http://sse.org.au/ing-direct-offers-100000-crowdfunding-initiative/ [accessed January 15, 2015]

Seyfang, G. and Smith, A. (2007). "Grassroots Innovations for Sustainable Development: Towards a New Research and Policy Agenda," *Environmental Politics*, 16(4), 584–603.

INDEX

INDEX